Making Winter

For Andy, Evie, Rose and Minnie,
and for the people who told me I could.

Making Winter

A Creative Guide for Surviving the Winter Months

Emma Mitchell

First published in Great Britain in 2017 by LOM Art, an imprint of
Michael O'Mara Books Limited
9 Lion Yard
Tremadoc Road
London SW4 7NQ

A CIP catalogue record for this book is available from the British Library.

Papers used by Michael O'Mara Books Limited are natural, recyclable
products made from wood grown in sustainable forests. The manufacturing
processes conform to the environmental regulations of the country of origin.

ISBN: 978-1-910552-65-0 in hardback print format
ISBN: 978-1-910552-66-7 in ebook format

1 2 3 4 5 6 7 8 9 10

www.mombooks.com

Interior and cover photography and illustration by Emma Mitchell
Cover design by Claire Cater
Designed and typeset by Claire Cater

This book contains lifestyle advice including instructions and recipes.
Appropriate caution should be used and safety clothing should be worn when
working with a naked flame or any sharp objects. Neither the publisher nor the
author can accept any liability for any injury or loss that may occur as a result of
information given in this book.

Printed and bound in China.

Contents

Introduction

When the days start to shorten, I eye the trees warily. At the first yellowing leaf, I grumble inwardly. Once the first branches are bare, I have an urge to swaddle myself in cosy textiles. In the bleak, incessant, slate-grey days of midwinter, I peer at the sky with contempt and beadily watch the progress of the bulb shoots in the garden, egging them on until snowdrop time. Despite the presence of that twinkly celebration right in the middle of it, winter and I have a strained relationship. At best, I feel a little flat, but on very dreary days it makes me feel rather gloomy. Most years, as summer ends, I wish I were a grizzly bear and could eat all the cake and sandwiches in the picnic baskets of Yellowstone National Park, build up a pleasing layer of blubber, dig a large but snug hole and go to sleep until the warmer weather draws me out. However, as a human being, it might be better to devise rather more sociable ways of embracing the colder months.

Serotonin. It's a peculiar word and sounds rather like a sort of tech start-up or perhaps a pond-dwelling creature. In fact, it is one of the compounds that carry signals between one nerve cell and another in our brains. Its role in our day-to-day life is quiet, unseen yet hugely significant. The presence and quantity of the neurotransmitters in our brains are factors that contribute to our outlook, our energy levels and our urges to eat and sleep. Serotonin is one that directly affects the way we feel, and when bursts

of it are released, we feel energized and our mood is lifted. This compound also influences our immune system. When its levels are lowered it can lead to feelings of sluggishness, listlessness and anxiety, and can even affect the way in which we fight infection.

As the calendar shifts beyond autumn, the intensity of the sunlight available diminishes, as does the number of daylight hours. Sunlight has been shown to have a direct effect on the levels of serotonin in the human nervous system, and if the sunlight is more intense, the effect is more pronounced; during the winter months we tend to spend more time indoors, which can lead to feeling rather Eeyore-ish. One way to fend off the dark forces is to gather as much light into the eyes – and so serotonin into the neurons – as possible, by venturing out on walks.

Apart from the early brief blaze from dying leaves, the landscape looks rather drained of colour once summer is over. The view from many windows becomes strongly monochrome and shades of brown predominate. Green is less prevalent, and vibrant yellows, reds and blues are almost non-existent in the countryside and garden during winter. There is evidence that the sight of yellow and red trigger mood-boosting changes in our neurotransmitters, so it is little wonder that many people experience less *joie de vivre* during the winter months.

In the UK, it is estimated that around a third of adults are affected in some way by the decrease

in daylight hours and colour during the winter,[1] and this is a common pattern around the world. In the mildest cases, mood and energy levels can droop somewhat, but for around eight percent of people winter can cause a transient depression known as Seasonal Affective Disorder (SAD).

There are, fortunately, ways of fighting the effects of sunshine's elusiveness. Light boxes that provide a spectrum similar to sunlight are effective at lifting mood, as are standard treatments for depression. However, in recent years, I discovered that crafts and creativity helped to replace the spring in my step.

I started an online creative diary in 2008 and noticed that I felt somewhat less like an irascible hibernating bear on days when I had made something by hand, or baked, and that this effect was especially noticeable during winter. A year or two later, I learned to crochet, began to meet with friends once a week for yarncraft and cake, and discovered that this was a source of solace in the long winter evenings. I found myself reaching for my crochet on especially dreary days and that the repetitive, aesthetically pleasing process of making loops into stitches – which grew into soft blankets and scarves – absorbed my mind and lifted my mood. Baking a cake would bring a feeling of wellbeing that seemed to counter the flat fatigue that lurks during the greyest of days.

My anecdotal findings that creative activity can lift mood during winter are beginning to be supported by scientific research. It seems that yarncraft can lead to a relaxation or meditation-like response similar to that induced by yoga,[2] and one study has shown that meditation increases the levels of dopamine, another neurotransmitter that is associated with elevated mood.[3] Knitting leads to improved feelings of wellbeing and this effect is markedly increased when it takes place within a group of people.[4] Whipping up a pair of mittens could perhaps make the glass feel more full again.

Crocheting a Day-Glo, rainbow-striped onesie, climbing into it and staring at your reflection in a mirror for four months may be a step too far, but the experience of visiting a yarn shop, with its beautiful skeins arranged in colour-coordinated ombré groups, and the odd flash of vermilion or mustard, could be the vivid flowering meadow of the winter. Merino replaces marigolds. Astrantias give way to the softest pink alpaca. The colours of yarn, fabric, paint palettes and printing ink, and the creative process of making something with any of these, can replace the bursts of neurotransmitters released when you walk round a sun-drenched garden in full bloom in summer.

Making things during winter is a cunning strategy to help replace the feel-good brain chemicals that may falter during these dingier months. Add to this the joy of baking, the thrill of a chocolate fondant made in five minutes, the snugness of a home-made shawl and the deep satisfaction of meeting with friends to make some or all of the above, and the result is a delicious, cosy, baked, yarny toolkit with which to tackle winter's onslaught.

This is a creative survival guide to winter, a means to embrace the drab days and fill them with wrist warmers and baked goodness. Grab your crochet hooks, yarn and cocoa powder. Onwards into the cold …

1. http://www.theweathercompany.com/SAD%20research%20UK and http://www.independent.co.uk/life-style/health-and-families/health-news/seasonal-affective-disorder-1-in-3-people-suffer-from-sad-9814164.html
2. http://esource.dbs.ie/bitstream/handle/10788/1586/ba_croghan_c_2013.pdf?sequence=1
3. https://www.ncbi.nlm.nih.gov/pubmed/11958969
4. http://bjo.sagepub.com/content/76/2/50.abstract

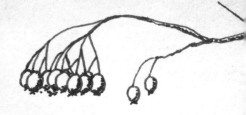

Nature as Nurture

I find the urge to stay indoors during autumn and winter to be almost overwhelming. My instinct is to light a fire, swaddle myself in blankets and quilts and feast on carbohydrates until the mercury starts to rise, a little like a hedgehog with a penchant for patchwork. However, as admirable as this plan is, I know that venturing outdoors for an hour or two can lift the spirits and actually enhance a wintry nest.

It doesn't matter how low the light levels might be on a grey autumnal or winter's day, allowing sunlight into your eyes by going outside for a walk causes an increase in serotonin in the brain, and a daily boost in its levels can help stave off the threat of feeling down. Similarly, a brisk stride around the park diminishes the stress hormone cortisol while boosting serotonin further. Simply being in a green space can alter levels of mood-boosting neurotransmitters.[1] Add to this the plum blondies you may have

taken with you, and the soothing activities you'll be embarking upon when you return with the makings of a new craft project, and suddenly the walk is transformed into something pleasantly medicinal, shifting your neurotransmitter dial towards joy.

Seed heads snipped from an obliging hedgerow, fallen cones, empty snail shells and feathers picked up on a walk may not be as colourful and verdant as spring and summer nature finds, but they are subtly beautiful and are especially cheering after Christmas decorations have been taken down. Using field guides to identify and label what you've found is a gentle, meditative task and the small repetitive movements of hand and eye made as you draw a feather or cluster of seeds can help to increase levels of feel-good neurotransmitters still further. Research has shown that having plants in your home can boost mood.[2] Small reminders

of nature walks you have taken may play the same role, so bring home any small treasures you may find.

If you live far away from a park, wood or patch of waste ground then a trip to a winter garden, where planting is designed to be at its best during the colder months, can be a reminder that all is not brown, dead and crispy. Winter-flowering and berry-laden trees and shrubs such as *Viburnum bodnantense*, *Prunus subhirtella* (winter-flowering cherry), *cotoneasters* and *Callicarpa* can be laden with colour even in midwinter and beyond. These gardens are often filled with the flame reds and oranges of dogwood (*Cornus*) stems and the frosty-looking, thorny branches of ornamental blackberries.

Casting your eyes over this colour and growth, followed by a large scone with jam and cream or a slab of brownie in the tea room, will lead to winter flower and cake-based contentment.

1.http://www.motherearthnews.com/nature-and-environment/ importance-of-nature-zm0z15djzcom and http://www.bbc. co.uk/news/science-environment-25682368 and http://www. newyorker.com/tech/elements/what-is-a-tree-worth
2.http://krex.k-state.edu/dspace/handle/2097/227

Preserving Autumn Leaves

In autumn and early winter, chlorophyll, the green pigment within leaves, is absorbed back into the plant, and the red and yellow pigments called anthocyanins and carotenoids that are present all year round are unmasked. The leaves of some species such as maples, Boston ivy and cherry are jewel-like and beautiful, and I always have a strong urge to gather them from the ground and bring them home. The problem is that they dry up quickly and become crispy or begin to decay. I've often wondered about capturing the colour of those leaves somehow: a way of putting them into suspended animation for later in the winter, when outdoor natural colour is scarce.

Last year, I tried preserving leaves and berries in glycerine for the first time. They remained pliable and shiny, and didn't fade or dry: leafy joy! When certain large flowers, autumn leaves or berries are submerged in a glycerine solution, some of the water in their cells is replaced by glycerine molecules, which remain in the cells, preventing further drying or loss of pigment. This method may take several days but the effort required is minimal and it can result in a collection of beautifully preserved plant materials for use in creative projects.

Materials

Your chosen leaves, berries or flowers
Glycerine (found in the baking
    aisle or at the chemist)
Water
Baking trays, roasting tins or a tall jug
A couple of pebbles and string or twine (if
    preserving large flowers or berry clusters)

Leaves to Look Out For
Boston ivy
Maple (including field maple)
Birch
Ivy
Cotoneaster
Some varieties of cherry

You can use this method to preserve several leaves attached to one twig or slender branch from species like birch and field maple, whose leaves are relatively small.

Large flowers, such as hydrangeas, and slender branches with berries, such as hawthorn or rose, can also be preserved in this way.

Step by Step

1 Make a solution of 1 part glycerine to 2 parts water.

2 To preserve individual leaves, pliable stems or branches, pour the glycerine solution into a large roasting tray, submerge the stems and/or leaves, and find a way to keep them submerged in the solution. Placing a baking tray on top of the stems and leaves works well.

3 To preserve large flowers such as hydrangeas or clusters of berries, pour your glycerine solution into a jug, tie a pebble or two to the base of the stem of the hydrangea or berry cluster with string or twine, and lower into the liquid. The pebble(s) will ensure that your foraged treasure will stay submerged during the preservation time.

4 Leave your leaves/berries/flowers in their solution for at least two days but no more than four.

5 Remove your finds from the glycerine solution, rinse them briefly in water, then dry them by blotting with kitchen towel or leave them out overnight at room temperature.

6 That's it! Put your leaves in a vase (don't add water) or use them in creative projects. They last an incredibly long time. Mine from last autumn are still going strong.

Tips

You could use the leaves to trim natural wreaths (see page 76 for details), add them to nature collections you might be making through the winter, or sketch or paint them (see pages 33 and 96).

Fennel Cowl

As autumn approaches, umbellifer seed heads are a common sight in Fenland hedgerows. Umbellifers are wild flower annuals with flowers shaped like tiny upturned umbrellas, and include cow parsley, wild carrot (Queen Anne's lace), wild fennel and pignut.

This cowl pattern uses clusters of double treble crochet stitches to form an umbellifer-like motif. It echoes the fennel seed heads I see in the wood behind our cottage which appear in huge drifts of exquisite lacy blooms in spring and summer. This cowl is perfect for wearing out on cold days, as the fabric formed is dense and will keep out the chill. I have used Malabrigo Mecha chunky in Polar Morn, a beautiful grey-blue colourway that echoes frozen ponds and snow-laden clouds.

Materials

1 skein of chunky weight yarn (approx. 100g)
6mm hook (size J-10)
Scissors
Yarn needle for weaving in ends

Abbreviations & Definitions

ch chain
sk skip
sp space
slst slip stitch
dc double crochet
tr treble crochet
yo yarn over
st/s stitch/es
htr half treble crochet: yo, insert hook, yo, pull through, yo, pull through all 3 loops on hook
dtr double treble: yo twice, insert hook, yo, pull through, [yo, pull through 2 loops] three times
shell work 9 dtr in one stitch

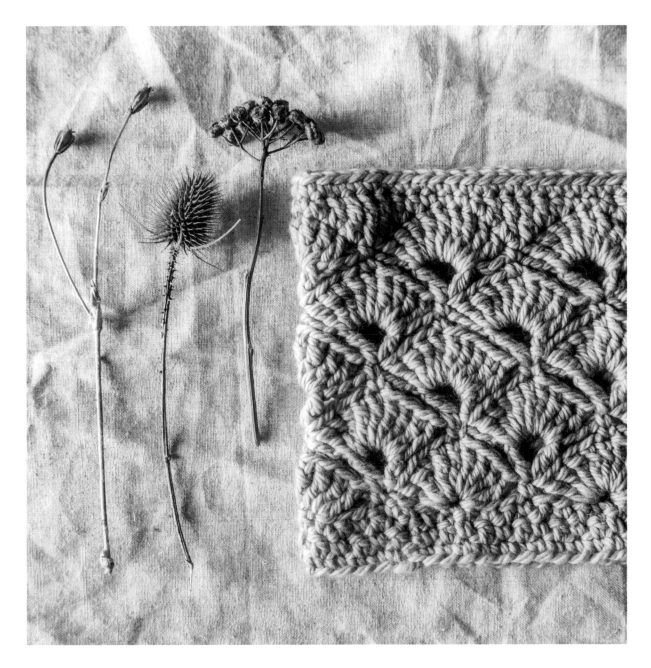

Pattern

To begin, work 80 foundation chain quite loosely. Join with a slst to work in the round, being careful not to twist the chain.

Round 1: ch1 (does not count as st throughout), dc in each st to end, join with a slst in first dc.
Round 2: ch1, *dc1, tr1; repeat from * to end, join with a slst in first dc.
Round 3: ch1, *tr1, dc1; repeat from * to end, join with a slst in first tr.
Round 4: ch1, *dc1, sk 3 sts, shell in next st, sk 3 sts; repeat from * 9 more times, join with a slst in first dc.
Round 5: ch4, dtr1 in first dc (at base of ch4), *ch3, dc1 in 5th dtr of shell, ch3, (dtr1, ch1, dtr1) in next dc; repeat from * 8 more times, ch3, dc

in 5th dtr, do not slst but continue to Round 6.
Round 6: Make shell in space between 4ch and first dtr of Round 5, dc in next dc, *shell in next 1ch sp, dc in next dc; repeat from * 8 more times, do not slst but begin next round after working final dc.
Rounds 7–12: Repeat Rounds 5 and 6, 3 more times. Note: the beginning of round will shift to the right as you work.
Round 13: ch4 (counts as 1dtr), sk st at base of ch, dtr1, tr1, htr1, *dc3, htr1, tr1, dtr3, tr1, htr1; repeat from * 8 more times, dc3, htr1, tr1, dtr1, join with a slst to top of 4ch.
Round 14: ch1, dc in each st to end, join with a slst in first dc.
Break yarn and weave in ends.

Plum, Orange and Ginger Blondies

When I emerge from the house during winter, I'm always surprised by how good it feels. Nestling next to an open fire is all very well, but even when there's an incessant drizzle wafting drearily from the sky, being outdoors can be uplifting. If you're off on a walk, though, a day with that almost transparent, liquid winter sunshine is the best choice. Taking with you a chunk or two of something delicious to eat on the way will make the walk even lovelier. Imagine stopping for a few minutes in the clearing of a wood and eating one of these fruity, citrus-fragranced blondies while sitting on a bench in the winter sunshine. Sunshine boosts mood and so do carbohydrates, especially when laced with plums steeped in sloe gin, ginger and orange. It's a recipe to put a spot of spring in your step.

Ingredients

180g (6oz) (plus 2 tsp for the plums) of golden caster sugar or light soft brown sugar (if you've been storing a vanilla pod or two in it, so much the better)

4 large eggs

225g (8oz) butter, melted

150g (5oz) plain flour

1 orange, finely zested

Pinch of salt

3 plums, de-stoned and chopped into pieces approx. 1cm (½in.) cubed

2 tbsp sloe gin (optional)

1 ball of ginger preserved in syrup, finely chopped (optional)

Makes 8–12 chunks

Step by Step

1 Line a 20cm (8in.) square or rectangular (around 20–25 x 30–35cm or 8 x 12in.) baking tin with baking parchment and preheat your oven to 180°C/350°F/gas 4.

2 If you have a little extra time, place your chopped plums in a pan with the sloe gin and 2 tsp of sugar, and bring to a simmer for a minute or so while stirring gently. This is to allow the gin to infuse into the plums, the sugar to dissolve and (some of) the alcohol to evaporate. Drain the sloe gin syrup into a cup. If time is tight, or booze isn't your thing, the chopped plums will still taste delicious in the blondies without their gin treatment.

3 Place the sugar and eggs in a large bowl and whisk together for 3 minutes or so to create a light, voluminous mousse.

4 Carefully pour the melted butter into the mixture while continuing to whisk. Ensure that the butter is well combined before moving on to the next step.

5 Fold in the flour, baking powder, orange zest and salt, then whisk again to add a little more air.

6 Add the plums and chopped ginger (if using), and fold into the mixture carefully to distribute them evenly.

7 Pour the mixture into the lined tin and shake gently to level it. Then, if you fancy a bit of decoration, you can add slices of plum to the top. Bake for 25–30 minutes or until a skewer comes out clean.

8 Allow the blondies to cool, cut into squares and either take them with you on a walk or serve with a dollop of your favourite dairy product and a drizzle of the sloe gin syrup on top for a fancy-ish pudding. Alternatively, save the small glass of plum-infused sloe gin and enjoy it in private.

Silver Fossil Pendant

Silver clay is an astonishing substance, made from the finely ground silver recovered from the printed circuit boards within broken electrical devices. It can be used to capture the tiniest details from nature by pressing leaves, silicone moulds made from fossils, seedpods or acorns into its surface. No expensive or high-tech equipment is required to make jewellery from silver clay; a gas hob or camping stove/trangia, a piece of steel gauze, metal polishing pads and a small brush are all that is needed to begin at home. The basic tools and materials aren't very expensive, and you can acquire these from craft shops on the high street or online.

There is a moment after you have just fired your pendant, plunged it into water to cool it and begun to polish off the silver oxide, when many people gasp. I've even witnessed some becoming a little tearful at this point. A piece of rather drab, unpromising-looking clay is transformed into a piece of pure silver, and a beautiful piece of jewellery. It's a modern version of alchemy.

Materials

For the pendant:
2–4g silver clay (Art Clay Silver 650 Slow Dry)
Sharp straight edge knife
Small plastic rolling pin (a thick marker pen also works well)
Plain, flat glazed tile (do not make your pendant on a tiled worktop)
Drop of cooking oil
Greaseproof paper
Selection of leaves
Headpin (length of wire with tiny sphere on its end used in beading techniques)
Circular or leaf-shaped cutter 2–3cm (1in.) in diameter (the narrow end of a wide piping bag nozzle works, too)
Baby wipe or piece of dampened kitchen towel folded several times
Long tweezers
Gas hob or camping stove
Firing gauze

For the finish:
Small metal wire polishing brush
Pro polishing pads from Metal Clay Ltd (optional)
Old aluminium knitting needle for burnishing (optional)
A solution of bleach (1 part bleach, 3 parts water) (optional)
Small amount of water in a saucer

For the necklace:
Silver-plated or sterling jump ring 5–6mm in diameter (3- or 4-gauge)
Silver-plated or sterling fine chain necklace
Pliers

Step by Step

1 Ensure your tile is clean and dry, then apply a drop of oil to it and rub it into a small area. This will prevent your silver clay from sticking. Cut a piece of greaseproof paper around 10cm (4in.) square and have it ready near your tile.

2 Use your knife to cut a piece of clay from your pack about 1 x 1cm (½ x ½in.) and place it on your oiled surface. Rewrap the remainder of your clay carefully in its original packaging to keep for your next project.

3 Roll out your piece of silver clay into a roughly circular shape, as evenly as you can, until it is just bigger than 2cm (1in.) in diameter. Try not to roll it thinner than 1–2mm (¹⁄₁₆in.)or your pendant will be very fragile at the smoothing stage.

4 Place the reverse side of your leaf onto the silver clay, ensuring its stalk extends beyond the edge of the rolled-out clay a little – this will make it easier to remove the leaf from the clay later. Carefully, so as not to shift the position of the leaf in the clay, place your greaseproof paper on top of it. Rub the leaf gently through the greaseproof paper with the pad of your finger, especially along the leaf's central vein, to impress the detail of the veins into the clay.

5 Lift the greaseproof paper off the clay, carefully grasp the end of the leaf stalk, and peel the leaf away from the clay. If you prefer the outline of your pendant to remain organic and just as you rolled it out, then go on to step 6. If you'd rather a perfectly circular pendant, then press the cutter into the clay in your chosen position. Alternatively, a leaf shape imprinted with real leaf veins can also be very effective. Hold the cutter in place and use your knife to remove the uneven edges. Roll the left over pieces into a ball and place them back into your silver clay package to use another time.

6 Poke your headpin into the silver clay around 2–3mm (¹⁄₈in.) down from the top of your fossil pendant using the ball end. Ensure the headpin is pressed right down through the clay to the hard surface beneath. Then move the wire end of the headpin in tiny circles to open the hole up. This creates a hole through which to insert your jump ring, which will allow you to hang your pendant from a chain.

7 Use the pad of your finger to gently and carefully flatten any raised areas around the jump ring hole you have made.

Leaves to Look Out For

Leaves with prominent veins make the best fossil pendants. Sage and salvias usually keep some leaves during winter, as do primulas and primroses, and on the backs of their leaves are beautiful filigree patterns of veins that lend themselves perfectly to this project. Alpine thyme, ferns, heathers and fir species with small needles are also excellent options.

8 Put your pendant, still attached to its tile, into the oven at 80–100°C/175°F/gas 1–2 for 15–20 minutes. This will remove all the moisture from your pendant, preventing any water in your design from boiling when you fire it, which would ruin its surface. Allow it to cool.

9 After drying, the fossil pendant should detach easily from the tile, leaving a flat back. Hold it very carefully, supporting the edge with your fingers (it can be rather brittle at this stage, like a very thin biscuit). Use the folded baby wipe or damp kitchen towel to remove any ragged or sharp pieces from around the edge. Smooth the rough pieces of clay away gently. If too much force is applied to the dry clay at this stage, it can snap or split.

10 Hold the pendant up to the light and ensure that you can see through the hole you have made near the top. If not, place it on a hard surface and very carefully use the headpin to open the hole a little more.

11 Place your firing gauze over one of the hobs of your gas cooker or on to your camping stove. Light the gas, turn it up to its highest level and let the gauze heat up until one or more areas become red hot.

12 Carefully use your tweezers to place the pendant on one of the red-hot areas of the gauze. Take care when placing the pendant onto the gauze for firing and when quenching as it will be very hot.

13 Watch carefully – a wisp of smoke followed by a flame will rise up from your pendant. This flame is the cotton and paper fibres within the clay burning off to leave fine silver. Do not turn the gas flame off. Once the flame from your pendant has died down, leave the gas flame burning beneath your pendant for another 3–5 minutes before turning it off. This ensures that all the cotton fibres burn away completely, leaving pure silver.

14 Let the pendant cool for 5 minutes on the gauze. It should look matte white – this is

silver oxide on the surface. Hold your pendant firmly and use your wire brush to polish the oxide away, to reveal the silver underneath. (This is a very exciting moment!) Be persistent with your brush. The pendant is now made of silver – you don't have to be careful, as it is no longer fragile.

15 You can leave your pendant with a matte, brushed silver finish, or you can use your Pro polishing pads to generate a mirror shine on the surface.

16 Experiment with burnishing the surface by using the edge of an old aluminium knitting needle to create areas of very high shine that contrast well with the matte finish.

17 If you'd like to highlight the tiny details of your pendant even further, then immerse it in the bleach solution for 1–2 minutes. Rinse in your saucer of water and repeat the polishing and burnishing process in steps 15 and 16.

18 Use your pliers to open the silver jump ring, slip the ring through the hole you made at the top of your pendant and thread your necklace or bracelet chain through the ring. Close the jump ring using your pliers.

19 That's it – your silver fossil pendant is finished. Try on your necklace and get ready to bask in the inevitable slew of compliments.

Tips

If the clay begins to dry out a little while you are making your pendant, don't worry. Moisten your finger very, very slightly in water, touch it onto the clay and it should become soft again, revitalizing the surface. If you discover that the clay has dried out while in storage, then place it in a small ziplock bag, add a couple of drops of water and knead the water into the clay. Continue kneading until the clay is uniformly soft (this may take up to 20 minutes) then reuse.

Nature Diaries

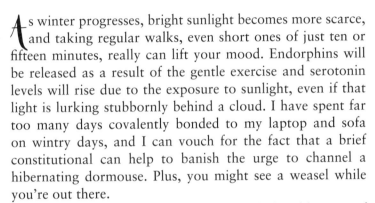

lychnis

Streptopelia

Hedera

As winter progresses, bright sunlight becomes more scarce, and taking regular walks, even short ones of just ten or fifteen minutes, really can lift your mood. Endorphins will be released as a result of the gentle exercise and serotonin levels will rise due to the exposure to sunlight, even if that light is lurking stubbornly behind a cloud. I have spent far too many days covalently bonded to my laptop and sofa on wintry days, and I can vouch for the fact that a brief constitutional can help to banish the urge to channel a hibernating dormouse. Plus, you might see a weasel while you're out there.

One way to stop regular walks from feeling like part of a very worthy Victorian health regime is to record what you see while you're outdoors. Taking photographs on your phone is an excellent way to mark and observe the subtle changes that occur as winter progresses. Writing down and even drawing what you find each week helps to transform a walk from an obligation, easily avoided, into something to savour. Alternatively, you could make a nature collection by arranging and labelling your finds. This practice harks back to the collections of nineteenth-century naturalists and their cabinets of curiosity. For me it echoes the displays in my favourite museums, where the faded copperplate labels, many written in the nineteenth and early twentieth centuries, are as beautiful as the exhibits themselves.

I remember one dank December day last year when I wrenched myself away from the cosiness of our cottage. I

Salix caprea

Cepaea nemoralis

Acer pseudoplatanus

walked to the edge of the village, where there is a tiny bridge over a Roman lode, a canal-like waterway that was used to travel between Ely and the surrounding settlements by boat and barge. The sycamore branches were bare and I stood for a few minutes looking at the patterns they made against the grey sky. Then, at the corner of my vision, I saw a quick flurry of animal movement on the opposite bank of the lode. I assumed it was a cat or perhaps a rat, but as my eyes shifted focus from sky to ground, I realized that the movement was snaking and that the animal was long, slender and very quick. It was a weasel and it seemed to writhe through the tired winter foliage on the lode bank as it made its way under the bridge. I had only ever seen a weasel a few times in my life and never at such close quarters. I was so glad that I'd parted from

the soft furnishings and come on my walk. I felt privileged to have seen this animal.

Most of the nature observations I make on my winter walks are more mundane than watching a weasel scamper among ivy, but they are no less uplifting. I often have to drive across the Fen to pick up silver clay supplies from a neighbouring village. The road is lined with young oak trees and in October the acorns begin to ripen and fall. Last year, my eldest daughter and I set about collecting acorns for my workshops (I teach people how to cast them in silver). The range of colours of the acorns we found was astonishing – from almost yellow, through all the browns you could conceive of to a bright acid green. I brought them home and recorded them on Instagram, which has, since 2015, become a sort of nature journal for me.

It's not too late to learn a little more about the wild birds, plants and specimens we may discover on a walk. Early winter is a good time to begin – there will still be the bright leaves of cherry, jewel-like rosehips and berries, umbellifer seed heads, acorns, moulted feathers and the cones of alder, larch and pine to find. A field guide or two will help you to identify species of land snails and to tell whether you have found a cow parsley or hogweed seed head (giant hogweed causes skin burns and looks remarkably like its innocuous cousins: avoid seed heads that are on stalks over 2m/6ft tall and as big as a cat). Getting outside, recording what you see, bringing home small finds, and drawing and annotating them can be part of an uplifting and soothing daily project that lasts throughout the winter.

Croodle

Danish winters are especially long, with sunlight a rare commodity. But rather than experiencing a nationwide dingy gloom that might be expected in such a dark season, a sort of joy descends on the country during winter. Hygge (pronounced 'hooga') is cosiness, candlelight, meeting and eating with friends. In the last two years, hygge has become a bit of a trend but there is a word to denote this feeling of cosy wellbeing in many countries. In Germany, *gemütlichkeit* means warmth, good cheer and belonging. In Sweden, *gemytlig* is the equivalent term, and the Italian word for this feeling, often used in winter, is *comodità*. The closest British word, one that has fallen into misuse, is 'croodle', which means nestling together in the manner of chickens in a cosy coop.

For many, a period of self-deprivation and almost punishment for the indulgences of Christmas descends in the New Year. Thoughts turn to trainers and the juice squeezed from a vegetable. These have their merits, but Danes hold little truck with austere regimes in winter. The weather and lack of sunlight are seen as sufficiently trying without inflicting a joyless stricture based around pulped turnip and rare grains. A crucial part of the Danish approach to winter is kindness to oneself – finding the means to brighten winter days by seeking comfort and delicious food. If that food contains butter and sugar and is deep-fried to enhance its allure then so much the better. A little indulgence is part of the Scandi winter plan.

In recent winters there has been a permanent fixture in my diary every Thursday night. I meet with two friends and we make things together. Essential ingredients for this small but excellent event are an open fire, a warming, usually hedgerow-based liqueur, refined carbohydrates (usually cake) and the particular yarn-based or sewing project each of us is working on at the time. We often bring slippers and sometimes

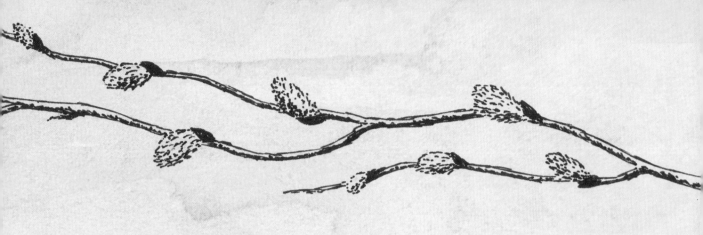

pyjama bottoms to one another's houses, and nestling under rugs is a regular occurrence. The most joyous part of craft night, though, is the companionship of these two excellent women. For us, making things by hand is not a passing fad, it's as essential as eating. Without it, life is rather drab and that satisfied feeling of donning your latest hat and knowing that you made it yourself is enhanced when you show it to friends.

I believe that the positive feelings caused by making things stems from the evolutionary benefits to ancient man of being able to fashion clothing out of animal skins or spin a fleece into yarn and knit or weave it into blankets or garments. People who were skilled at sewing, weaving, knitting, weapon-making, carving or shelter-building were more likely to survive the colder weather. The feelings of wellbeing that are experienced when we make a hat or even a pile of logs for the fire are inherited from our ancestors. Equally, the very basis of our success as a species is locked into our ability to cooperate and share our collective knowledge, and so it is no wonder to me that when several people gather together to make things in a group there is an extra feeling of rightness and wellbeing.

If getting together with friends is tricky for you, there are many craft communities online that you can join in with: knit-a-longs and crochet-a-longs happen regularly in ravelry groups or on blogs, and Twitter offers a wonderful opportunity to share your weekly progress to widespread crafty glee. I've included as many seasonal handmade projects in this book as I could fit between the covers and I hope that making them alone on a cold Saturday afternoon with the radio on might make a midwinter day lovelier. However, many of them could also be made with pals in close proximity to cake, conferring, I hope, even more comfort and cheer on dingy evenings.

Pantile Shawl

When I glance out of our bedroom window in November, I notice the swag-like patterns made by the 200-year-old interlocking terracotta tiles (known as pantiles) on the roof of a cottage across the village green. Sometimes, winter brings out the details of buildings that may be overshadowed by trees and flowers during warmer months. I confess that I thought of Florentine as well as Fenland roof tiles when I designed this shawl (sometimes my mind wanders to Tuscany on dreary afternoons).

The stitch I have used in this shawl uses stretches of chain and little picot loops to create an attractive open trellis- or tile-like pattern, but the holes are not so big as to prevent the fabric from keeping you warm on a wintry walk. Despite its intricate look, the pattern is deceptively simple. Beginners can tackle it without worrying about the calculus-like complexity of so many shawl patterns.

Perhaps my favourite element of this pattern is its meditative repetition. Once you have crocheted the simple repeat a few times, your fingers will become familiar with it and finger-yarn-brain autopilot takes over. It's a perfect pattern to make with friends on craft night, as you can discuss the historical accuracy of Poldark's trousers at the same time as hooking this up.

Materials

At least 2 skeins of chunky yarn.
  I used 4 skeins of Madelinetosh
  Home, in Smokestack
8mm hook (size L-11)
Scissors
Yarn needle for weaving in ends

Abbreviations & Definitions

ch chain
slst slip stitch
dc double crochet

If you're a beginner and would like to learn the basic crochet stitches, you can find full instructions on my website: silverpebble.net.

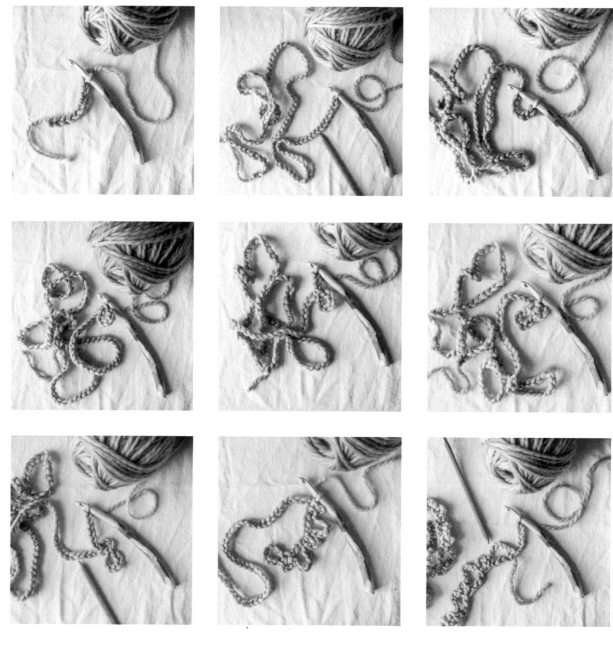

Pattern

Cast on multiples of 4 stitches plus 4. I made a foundation chain of 164. Drape this foundation chain around your shoulders and use the multiples of 4 stitches plus 4 guide to make it the length you choose.

Row 1: 1dc in 8th ch from hook, 3ch, 1 slst in dc just made (this creates a picot), *7ch, skip 3ch, 1dc in next ch, 3ch, 1 slst in dc just made (picot), repeat from * ending 1dc in last ch. Turn.
Row 2: 7ch, skip first 3ch, *1dc in next ch (4th of 7ch), picot, 7ch, skip [3ch, next dc, picot, 3ch], repeat from * ending 1dc in 4th of 7ch. Turn.

Repeat Row 2 ending: 1dc in 4th of 7ch. Continue adding rows to the shawl until it is the width you prefer. I made 20 rows after the initial foundation chain.

To finish: turn, 7ch, skip 3ch, dc in next ch, picot, break yarn and weave in ends.

Note: You can also use this pattern to make a beautiful scarf using a shorter foundation chain and fewer rows, or a denser shawl with smaller gaps by using aran or worsted yarn and a 5/6mm (US H/J 8/10) hook.

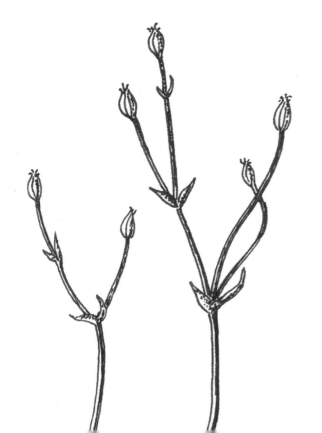

Apple and Caramel Chelsea Buns

They're the British version of a Danish pastry and were first invented in the Old Chelsea Bun House in London some time during the 1700s. The dough is enriched and often flavoured with lemon or spices; the classic filling is butter, brown sugar and dried vine fruits, and once baked, they're glazed to make glistening spirals of light bread dough drenched in toffee-ish flavours or icing.

My Chelsea bun recipe takes advantage of the availability of cooking apples during the colder months. There's something about the sharp yet sweet flavour of Bramleys that I associate with comfort and with winter. Stewed apple, sometimes with custard, was a regular pudding when I was small. Here the pairing of soft tangy apple with light bread dough and caramel is reassuring, filling and best eaten with a pot of tea.

This is not a speedy recipe – once you decide to reach for the ingredients it will be two hours or so before you can demolish your first bun – but the slowness of the process and the tantalizing anticipation is part of its joy. I find kneading and cutting buns from a batch of risen dough as soothing as making stitches with yarn, and between the gentle bursts of baking activity required to conjure your batch of appley spirals, I recommend retreating back into a book, a crochet project or a good film. It's a recipe that lends itself to a slower pace. It is a duvet for your taste buds – hygge in a bun.

Ingredients

For the dough:
40g (1½oz) butter
180ml (6fl oz) milk
500g (1lb 2oz) strong white bread flour
1 x 7g (¼oz) sachet of easy bake yeast
1 tsp salt
1 egg

For the apple caramel filling:
2 large cooking apples (choose a variety that breaks down during cooking), peeled and grated
75g (2½oz) soft brown sugar
50g (2oz) butter, melted
Good drizzle of golden syrup
Zest of a lemon

For the glaze:
8 tbsp of milk
6 tbsp of golden syrup (tip: oil the tablespoon before measuring out and it'll slip off the spoon much more easily)
Good pinch of salt

Makes 12 buns

Step by Step

1 Grease a 23cm (9in.) high sided baking tin generously and set aside.

2 Warm the butter and milk in a pan until the butter is just starting to melt. Then take it off the heat and let it sit while you measure out your dry ingredients. If the mixture gets too warm it may kill some of your yeast and impede the rise of your buns.

3 Put the flour, salt and yeast into a bowl, make a well in the centre, break the egg into it and pour in the butter/milk mixture, then stir with a table knife until all the ingredients come together into a uniform, rather sticky dough.

4 Knead the dough on a floured surface for 10 minutes.

5 Leave to rise in a clean, lightly oiled bowl covered by a clean tea towel in a warm place for an hour. This is the first proving stage.

6 Once you've grated your apples, put them in a sieve and give them a squeeze or press them with a wooden spoon to remove some of the juice.

7 Put the grated apple in a bowl, add all the other ingredients for your filling and mix together.

8 Once the dough has risen to twice its original size, roll it into a rough rectangle about 25 x 40cm (10 x 16in.), spread your filling on to its surface leaving a 2cm (1in.) space along the long edge furthest away from you, and roll the rectangle into a large sausage shape by starting at the long edge nearest to you and rolling away towards the far edge in the same way as you would if making a Swiss roll. 'Seal' the sausage by pinching the edge of the dough together with the main body of the sausage to prevent the filling from leaking out.

9 Cut your dough into quarters. Cut each quarter into three pieces to make twelve buns – they'll be about 3–4cm (1–2in.) wide – and place into your baking tin. Place them next to each other – if you push them together just a little, the final proving will result in a pleasing squareish shape with a spiral of filling: the classic Chelsea bun design.

10 Place the ends of the dough sausage into the tin to bake with the rest (just tuck them in around the edge). They'll be slightly small and hard but will still have some filling in and are very good dipped in a mug of tea or coffee.

11 Leave your buns to rise in their tin for half an hour. This is the final proving stage. Meanwhile, preheat your oven to 180°C/360°F/gas 4.

12 Bake your buns for 30–45 minutes or until they are a deep golden brown. I cover mine with a roof of foil after 15–20 minutes or so, as they brown quite fast and sometimes catch in my oven.

13 While they're baking, make the glaze: simply put the milk, salt and golden syrup into a pan, bring to the boil, then turn down the heat and allow to simmer very gently on a low flame for 2 minutes or so to thicken slightly. Don't leave your glaze on the hob unattended, and keep stirring it as it can sometimes separate.

14 Remove your buns from the oven and pour the glaze over the top while they're still warm. The glaze will soak into the dough and seep underneath the buns to form a delicious sweet-yet-sharp caramel sauce. Serve to friends or loved ones in triumph, with large mugs of tea, coffee or hot chocolate. Alternatively, hoard them all for yourself and eat them when everyone's out.

Home-made Firelighters

During winter, lighting candles or a fire at dusk is a reassuring ritual that harks back to our ancestors. Several thousand years ago, a fire would have been the only source of light in winter, and I believe that the feeling of homeliness and relief triggered by bringing light into a dark afternoon or early evening has its roots in human history.

A few minutes spent lighting candles or tea lights and placing them around your living room each evening really can lift a wintry mood – I speak from experience. If you're lucky enough to have an open fire then lighting it can be part of this ancient routine. These home-made firelighters can bring you slightly closer to the tinderboxes of previous centuries, when making and maintaining a flame required a certain amount of craft and resourcefulness. I have tested them, and they not only burn for several minutes, but they also add a subtle scent to a room if essential oil or dried orange peel is used to make them. A bag of the scented versions of these firelighters make a lovely present and the plain versions can also be used to light bonfires, campfires, fire baskets or barbecues.

Materials

Wax from a few old candle stubs
  or a bag of wax pellets from a
  craft shop (approx. 45g)
A few drops of essential oil (optional)
Saucepan of boiling water
Heatproof bowl with a diameter larger
  than that of your saucepan
Cotton wool balls
Baking parchment
Tongs or tweezers
Garden twine cut into 30cm (12in.) lengths
  (1 length of twine for each firelighter)
Dry twigs, pieces of dried orange peel,
  dried sycamore keys etc. (optional)
Matches

Makes about 15 to 20 fire lighters

Note: Most garden twines are treated with paraffin or something similar to prevent them from rotting while outdoors. Sniff the twine before you buy it. If it smells like paraffin, it's perfect for this project.

Step by Step

1 Melt the wax in the heatproof bowl by placing the bowl over a pan of boiling water. At this point you can add a drop or two of your favourite essential oil, if you fancy.

2 Fluff up the cotton wool balls a little to ensure there are lots of protruding fibres – these will be the 'tinder' that catch the flame from the match and carry it to the wax in the firelighter to cause a prolonged flame.

3 Lay a sheet of baking parchment on a level surface and then grip a cotton wool ball with your tongs or tweezers. Carefully dip it into the wax two or three times and place it on the parchment.

4 After a few minutes, when the wax has hardened, wrap your firelighter with one of the pieces of garden twine two or three times round the wax-coated cotton wool ball and tie the twine with a double knot. You can also tie on a decorative dried twig or two, or a piece of dried orange peel, if you feel so inclined or if you plan to give a bag of firelighters as a present. The twine will provide more fibres to carry the flame towards the wax.

5 Use two or three of your firelighters when lighting a fire, brazier, bonfire or barbecue, along with dried kindling or tinder and small logs or pieces of coal. Hold the match to the ends of the twine to light your firelighters.

Hawthorn Gin

Hawthorn is one of the most common shrubs growing in hedgerows and scrubland in temperate areas of Europe, America and Asia. It's a member of the rose family and, like most varieties of rosehips, hawthorn berries (also known as haws) ripen in September and October. Gathering them in order to make a delicious liqueur for consumption as winter gathers pace is no chore. There are often clear, crisp sunny days during autumn, and venturing out to gather haws can make an autumnal walk even lovelier.

This recipe can also be used to make delicately fragranced and deliciously sharp rosehip gin. Wild rosehips from hedgerows are perfect for this. It is best to avoid taking rosehips from neighbours' gardens in case of grumpy recriminations. However, offering a bottle of rosehip gin in return for this harvest seems like an excellent solution.

When the sun goes down and the weather is gruesome, find a cosy spot, light some candles, find a good book (this one would do very well indeed), pour a small glass of one of these fine home-made, hedgerow berry-infused liquids and nestle down. There will soon be a glow within and without.

Materials

One or more 500ml or 1lt
  (17 or 34fl oz) jars with lever seals
  e.g. Kilner or Weck (it's crucial that
  the jars are airtight when closed)
Sharp scissors
Funnel
Muslin, 1m (3ft.) square is
  more than enough

Ingredients

Hawthorn berries – enough to fill your jar(s)
Gin (supermarket own-brands are
  fine) – enough to fill your jar(s)
White or golden granulated or caster sugar
  – around 400g (14oz) for a 1l (34fl oz) jar
  and 200g (9oz) for a 500ml (17fl oz) jar

Note: The seeds inside the hawthorn berries can be poisonous, so don't be tempted to sample the berries.

50

Step by Step

1 Collect enough haw berries to fill the jar in which you plan to make your gin.

2 Wash the berries and, with a pair of sharp scissors, remove any stalks and dried remains of the flower from the end of each berry. As haws are quite small this can take some time, so pop a film or box set on or listen to the radio while you top and tail them.

3 While you are preparing your haws, you can sterilize your jar. If your jar has a rubber seal, remove it and put to one side. Set your oven to 140°C/275°F/gas 1, wash your jar in hot soapy water thoroughly, place it on a baking tray (preferably upside down) and put it in the oven for around 10 minutes, then remove from the oven and allow to cool. Try not to touch the inside of your jar before you make your gin. Boil the rubber seal for 10 minutes in a saucepan of water.

4 Once they're free of their stalks and flower remains, tumble a layer of haws into your jar around 3cm (1½in.) thick. Pour in around a quarter of your sugar.

5 Add another layer of haws, top with sugar and repeat this process until you have filled the jar. Now pour in your gin.

6 Once you've filled your jar to the top, seal it, upend carefully a couple of times in case air has become trapped between the haw berries, and then top up with more gin to minimize the gap between the surface of the gin and the lid.

7 Place your gin on a kitchen shelf out of direct sunlight or in a cupboard for 4–6 weeks. After this time the colour from the berries will have seeped into the gin resulting in a beautiful pink, rosé wine colour.

8 You can let the haws infuse further but sediment will begin to form at this stage as the berries break down, which can be difficult to remove. To avoid this, sterilize another sealable jar or bottle and place your funnel in the top and several layers of muslin into the funnel. Pour your hawthorn gin through the muslin in the funnel and into the second jar or bottle. Discard the berries.

9 Enjoy on its own while nestled under a blanket or with good-quality tonic water.

Hedgerow Bird Snacks

Sitting in a warm room watching birds through a window is immensely relaxing, and knowing that you have put food out to help them survive the coldest weeks of the year makes this even more satisfying. A record of the various species of bird that visit your area is the perfect addition to a regular nature diary and allows you to become familiar with the diversity of birdlife in your local patch. You may spot winter migrants or more timid species of birds that will emerge to feed when the ground is frosty and most of the wild berries have been eaten.

Many garden centres have a section dedicated to bird food and feeders, but making special snacks for your feathery visitors is not only easy, it also ensures that you know exactly what the birds are eating and can pack their snacks with nutritious ingredients. This recipe includes hawthorn berries and rosehips that I collected from the hedgerows in November, but if you make these later in the winter, when fewer wild berries are available, they can be replaced with currants, sultanas or dried cranberries.

You may need to wait several days or even weeks for your local birds to discover the berry snacks you have made, but as the cold weather begins to bite, food sources like this are essential for survival, so they will find your treats eventually.

Materials

Lard
Wild berries such as hawthorn and rosehips, or dried fruit
Wild bird seed
Porridge oats
Cheese (optional)
Saucepan of boiling water
Heatproof bowl with a diameter larger than that of your saucepan
Coconut halves (available online), small coconut-fibre plant pots or yoghurt pots
Garden twine

Step by Step

1 Weigh your lard – an average block weighs around 250g (9oz).

2 Measure out the same weight in total of berries, birdseed, oats and cheese, in whatever proportions you wish.

3 Melt your lard in a large heatproof bowl over a pan of simmering water.

4 Remove the bowl from the heat and add your berries, dry ingredients and cheese (if using) to the lard and blend well with a spoon.

5 Leave the mixture to cool until the lard becomes opaque but is still soft enough to spoon into the coconut halves, plant pots or yoghurt pots.

6 Meanwhile, poke a small hole in the bottom of your yoghurt pots or coconut-fibre plant pots with a pencil or small screwdriver (the coconut halves often come with a string already attached).

7 Cut a piece of garden twine around 25cm (10in.) long, fold it in half and tie a double knot to form a loop.

8 Push your loop of string through the hole in the pot so that the knot remains inside.

9 Fill as many of your containers as you can with your mixture and allow it to cool and solidify completely.

10 If you have used yoghurt pots, the plastic can be cut away and recycled before you hang your bird snacks outside.

11 Choose a spot in your garden at least 1.5m (5ft) off the ground that is tricky for cats and other predators to reach, and with some foliage nearby to shelter shy species of bird between visits to the feeding area.

12 Sit near a window with a warm drink and watch the birds feeding, record them in your diary and perhaps even sketch them.

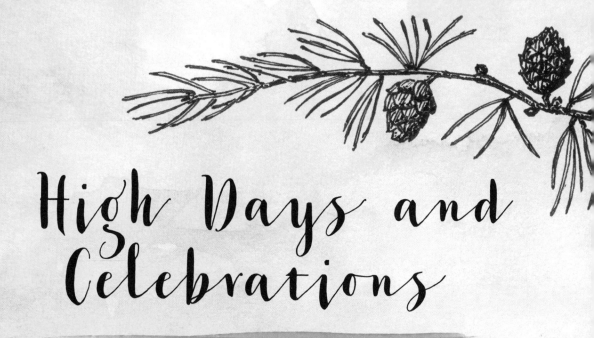

High Days and Celebrations

Sometimes, the festive period is so frenetic that the thought of making gifts or accessories by hand seems laughably implausible, and retreating into the wardrobe with a stiff hedgerow liqueur for a small cry and a cheering chunk of cake or a large slab of chocolate becomes the far wiser option. On certain days, those wardrobe-hiding, medicinal cake-eating urges must be fulfilled in order to stay sane during the final weeks before you-know-when.

However, making a few small gifts in the quiet of a Sunday afternoon not only allows a tick to be added (ever so slightly smugly) to the seemingly endless presents-and-preparation list, but an afternoon set aside to crochet a delicate lace necklace or make a wreath to hang on the door will confer a calmness that would hearten anyone in the face of the crazed Christmas crescendo. Venturing out to find hazel, willow, ivy or birch twigs to make into wreaths is an excellent excuse to go for a walk. Trees and green things, even if glimpsed briefly, will help to smooth away the angst of a deadline or a week so full of tasks that you'd quite like to be a squirrel that knows nothing about nativity plays or budgets.

These projects, particularly suited to pre-shindig preparations but pleasurable to do

at any point during winter, are quick to make yet still rather lovely, and the making itself is a therapeutic antidote to the seemingly incessant low-level stress that can lurk at this time of year. If you have an hour or two to spare, then the blackberry streusel cake is enough of a delicious showstopper to serve at any do, and the slow, steady process of making it while shut away in your kitchen can be a welcome baking escape. Time spent communing with caster sugar, butter and ground almonds can be almost as cheering as actually eating them.

Paper Leaf and Berry Bough

The festive season is the time when I have strong urges to line my house with beautiful handmade things. If I had the time, I would make everything, including hand-crocheted dungarees for the fairy on top of the tree. In reality, I manage to make two or three items each year – perhaps a decoration and a present or two. Time is tight, to-do lists are long, but making is soothing and can help to lower cortisol levels (the stress hormone), and papercraft is my particular favourite. This design is inspired by mind-bogglingly intricate paper-cuts of bucolic winter foliage and dioramas of scampering deer and badgers. I don't have time to spend three days cutting out a perfect paper rendering of an ancient hawthorn bush, so craft punches are an excellent short cut to conjuring beautiful decorations. These are like hole punches but with a single die, and used to cut a wide range of shapes out of paper or card. This design is inspired by wintry berries and leaves, takes about an hour to make and is not just for Christmas.

Materials

Thin white card (2 x A4 will be enough)
Leaf craft punch (the leaf should be 2–2.5cm [¾–1in.] in length)
Circle craft punch (the circle should be 1–2cm [½–¾in.] in diameter)
Silver-plated wire, 0.6mm in diameter (18 gauge)
Silver-plated wire, 1mm in diameter (22 gauge)
Wire cutters
Round-nosed pliers
Strong, clear paper glue
Pointed-nosed pliers
Piece of garden string, around 25cm (10in.) long

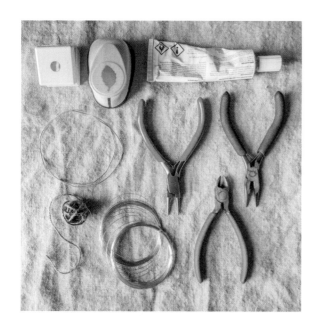

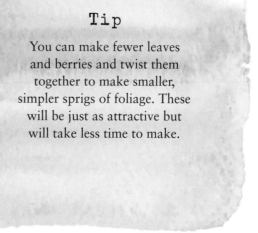

Tip

You can make fewer leaves
and berries and twist them
together to make smaller,
simpler sprigs of foliage. These
will be just as attractive but
will take less time to make.

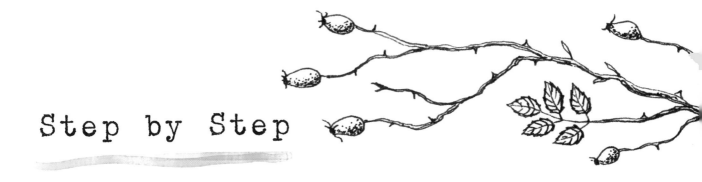

Step by Step

1 Use the leaf craft punch to cut out 36 leaves from the white card.

2 Then use the circle craft punch to cut out 30 circles.

3 Use your wire cutters to cut 33 lengths of the 0.6mm wire around 8cm (3in.) long, and make loops around 3–4mm in diameter at the end of each one by bending the wire around one of the 'noses' of your round-nosed pliers.

4 Make each berry by sandwiching a loop of wire between 2 circles of card with glue. Repeat to make the other 14 berries.

5 Make the 18 leaves the same way.

6 Bend the 1mm silver-plated wire into an arc around 12–15cm (5–6in.) long and make a loop at each end in the same way as described in step 3.

7 To attach the leaves to the wire, twist the wire extending from a leaf tightly around and around one end of the arc of the 1mm wire, so that the 0.6mm wire spirals around it several times. Then trim the excess wire off and squeeze the spiral of 0.6mm wire tightly onto the 1mm wire using your pointed-nosed pliers, so that the leaf doesn't slip.

8 Attach 2 more leaves in this way, followed by 3 berries.

9 Repeat this pattern until the whole of the 12–15cm (5–6in.) arc is filled with leaves and berries and the arc resembles a branch of winter foliage.

10 Tie your garden twine through each loop on the end of your wire arc and hang up your paper bough.

Crochet Lace Necklace

If a party invitation has just plopped into your inbox, or you have a particular friend who deserves a special gift, then this necklace is quick and immensely satisfying. Afterwards you will feel like an accomplished Victorian artisan having conjured what is, in effect, a tiny semicircle of crocheted lace. It sounds complicated and daunting, but it is actually a simple pattern using basic crochet techniques.

At first, it can seem tricky making crochet stitches on such a small scale, but once I had adjusted to the smallness, I found that I revelled in the miniaturization of the familiar patterns of stitches that are usually used to make crochet coasters or mandalas. The slight challenge of the scale is countered by the speed with which these necklaces can be made. I am far from nimble when crocheting with such a tiny hook (as I'm overdue a visit to the opticians), but it takes me only around twenty minutes to make the crochet part of this design. A whole afternoon sitting in front of *It's a Wonderful Life* and you could go into production and have a stall down the local Cats' Protection League craft fair.

Materials

Crochet cotton or linen thread (no more than 2m needed per necklace)
1.5mm (size 7) hook
Scissors
Yarn needle for weaving in ends
Fine-nosed pliers
Wire cutters
2 sterling or silver-plated jump rings, 6mm (¼in.) in diameter
Fine sterling or silver-plated chain, 45cm (18in.) long with links around 2–3mm (⅛in.) in diameter

Abbreviations & Definitions

ch chain
sk skip
sp space
slst slip stitch
dc double crochet
tr treble crochet
yo yarn over
st/s stitch/es
htr half treble crochet: yo, insert hook, yo, pull through, yo, pull through all 3 loops on hook

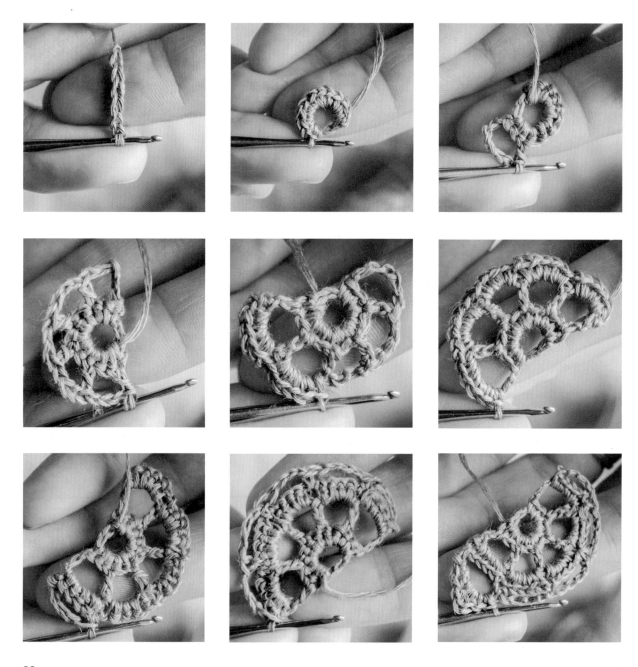

Pattern

To begin: make a slip knot and ch6, joining with a slst to form a ring.

Row 1: ch1 (does not count as st throughout), 10 dc into the ch ring. Turn.

Ensure you make your stitches close to one another, so that they form a semicircle rather than filling the whole ring.

Row 2: ch6 (counts as 1 tr and 3ch sp), sk 1 dc at base of chain, tr1 into next dc, *ch3, sk 1dc, tr1 into next dc; repeat from * 3 more times. Turn.
Row 3: ch1, sk 1tr, dc5 into 3ch sp, ch1, *dc5 into next 3ch sp, ch1; repeat from * 2 more times, dc5 into final 3ch sp. Turn.
Row 4: ch1, dc1, ch4, sk 4dc, dc1 into 1ch sp, *ch4, sk 5dc, dc1 into 1ch sp; repeat from * 2 more times, ch4, sk 4dc, dc1 into last dc. Turn.
Row 5: *ch1, sk 1dc, [dc1, htr2, tr1, htr2, dc1] into 4ch sp; repeat from * 4 more times. Break thread and weave in ends.

Step by Step

1 Iron your crochet semicircle on a setting suitable for your yarn.

2 Close your chain at the clasp, find the centre of the chain and use your wire cutters to cut the chain in half.

3 Use your pliers to open one of the jump rings slightly and thread the end of it through into the top right-hand corner of the crochet lace semicircle you have made, holding it so that the curved edge is pointing downward. Thread the same jump ring through one of the links on the end of your chain. Close the jump ring using your pliers.

4 Repeat step 3 with the second jump ring, attaching it to the other corner of your crochet lace semicircle.

5 Try on the necklace and admire your exquisite handiwork.

If you're a beginner and would like to learn the basic crochet stitches, you can find full instructions on my website: silverpebble.net.

Blackberry and Almond Streusel Cake

It's December. Friends are coming over and pudding is required. Cocooning yourself in your kitchen for a baking session may sound like hard work, but the making of this cake is gently reassuring, and at the end of it you'll be rewarded with an irresistible baked something, combining moist, rich cake filled with hedgerow fruit and an indulgent buttery, crumble-like topping. Cake and crumble in one: double joy-giving pudding prizes.

The hedgerows are blackberry-free zones during winter, but if you froze some earlier in the year or can find some frozen ones at a local farm shop or in a supermarket freezer, then they don't even have to be defrosted. In fact, adding the frozen berries directly to the cake mix before you put it in the oven means that they just soften and poach gently while the cake bakes, leaving them with just the right amount of bite when the cake is done.

This cake does have a special occasion sort of feel to it. The trickiest part of this recipe may be resisting eating a chunk of it before your visitors arrive.

Ingredients

For the cake:

200g (7oz) dry ingredients – I usually use:
  75g (2½oz) self-raising flour
  75g (2½oz) ground almonds
  50g (2oz) polenta
  (as long as it all adds up to 200g/7oz the proportions don't have to be accurate)
Zest of a lemon
1 tsp baking powder (level)
200g (7oz) golden caster sugar
200g (7oz) butter, softened
3 eggs
250–300g (9–11oz) fresh or frozen blackberries, plums, bullaces or raspberries

For the streusel topping:

50g (2oz) butter, cold
85g (3oz) plain flour
50g (2oz) demerara sugar
50g (2oz) pine nuts

Step by Step

1 Set your oven to 180°C/350°F/gas 4.

2 Line a 23cm (9in.) springform, loose-bottomed cake tin with baking parchment. I don't worry about origami – I just push a big (40cm/16in.) square of it into the tin quite well. When it's baked, it looks like a large muffin.

3 First, make the streusel topping by rubbing the butter into the flour and demerara sugar using your fingertips. When it looks like rough breadcrumbs, add the pine nuts, mix to distribute them and set aside.

4 Weigh out the flour, almonds, polenta and baking powder into another bowl along with the lemon zest and mix about a bit to blend. Set aside.

5 Weigh out the sugar and put into a large bowl or the bowl of your mixer.

6 Soften the butter (a minute or two in a microwave on a low setting) and scrape into the bowl with the sugar. Whisk with an electric hand whisk or your mixer until it's pale and fluffy.

7 Add one of the eggs and whisk to blend.

8 Add about a third of the flour mixture. Fold in thoroughly with a large spoon.

9 Repeat steps 7 and 8 twice more until no more eggs or flour mixture are left.

10 Add your blackberries (or plums, bullaces or raspberries) to the cake mix and stir them through. They will tend to clump, as they are frozen, so try to distribute them evenly throughout.

11 Tip the mixture into your lined cake tin, spread it to the sides and smooth the surface with a knife.

12 Wipe any splurges of cake mix away from the edge of the baking paper with a bit of kitchen towel. If you leave them, they will burn.

13 Sprinkle the streusel topping over the top of the mixture.

14 Bake for 40–50 minutes. Check it after 25 – if it's getting quite brown, cover it with foil and put it back in until it's been baking for 40 minutes.

15 After 40 minutes, stick a skewer in to check if it comes out clean. Otherwise, if the cake is coming away from the edges of the tin a tiny bit and springs back rather than wobbles when you poke it with your finger, it should be done. Put it back in the oven for another 5–10 minutes if it does not spring back.

16 Allow the cake to cool a little on a rack.

17 Eat with large dollops of dairy produce.

The Berry Cocktail

Sometimes a spot of booze is needed. And sometimes it needs to be sweet and prettily coloured and sipped while watching an old film on a chilly evening beneath a soft blanket. This recipe hits that spot. It's easy to make and perfect for drinking by the fire. The delicate pink or tawny colour is made from the old year's berries. You can use a nip of the hawthorn gin (see page 50) or a simple, delicious blackberry syrup that, with some brief simmering, distils the flavour of late summer so that you can taste it in your glass. All poetic thoughts aside, it will cheer you right up if there's a squall blowing outside, you dropped your purse in a puddle or you've yet to tackle your tax return. It is, like its namesake Mary Berry, reassuring and very lovely.

Ingredients

For the cocktail:
Sloe, damson, hawthorn or rosehip
   gin (see page 50 for recipe) or
   blackberry syrup (recipe below)
Your favourite white wine
A good tonic water
A few fresh berries (optional)

For the blackberry syrup:
350g (12oz) frozen blackberries
200g (7oz) golden caster sugar
Splash of water

Rubus fruticosus

Step by Step

Blackberry Syrup

1 To make a simple blackberry syrup, simmer the frozen blackberries with a good splash of water and the golden caster sugar until the fruit just breaks down and the juice is released. Don't allow it to become thick and jammy.

2 Strain the syrup through a sieve into a sterilized bottle and keep it in the fridge – you can save the pulp and eat it with your breakfast cereal.

Cocktail

1 Make your Berry Cocktail using the following ratios: 1 part fruit gin or blackberry syrup, 2 parts wine, 2 parts tonic water.

2 Add a few fresh berries to your glass for decoration, if you like.

3 Snuggle down and toast Mary Berry and the summer that was.

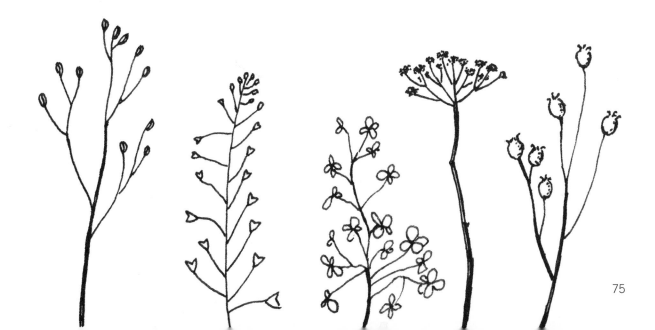

Woodland Wreaths

When the calendar moves beyond the beginning of December, many folk hang a wreath on their door. You can, of course, buy ready-made wreaths, which are usually constructed from offcuts of Christmas tree branches. Artificial ones are pretty common, too. While these shop-bought ones are festive, making your own wreath from branches and twigs you found on a walk is thrifty, satisfying and will help to boost your feel-good neurotransmitters by getting you outside and channelling your creativity. The wreaths you make will be natural, charming and often more delicate. You're also likely to be reluctant to put them away in the New Year. Wreaths made from foraged twigs are beautiful enough to be hung on doors and walls all year round.

The simplest wreaths of all – and perhaps the most elegant – consist of a single branch, stem or bundle of fine stems bent carefully into a circle and fixed in place with galvanized wire or garden twine. A collection of such smallish, delicate wreaths made this way and hung on a wall bring a lovely festive feel to a room and are easy on the pocket.

Materials

Secateurs
Plant material collected from your
    garden, local park or countryside*
Wire cutters
1–2mm (14 gauge) galvanized wire, garden
    twine
    or raffia

*A note about cutting material from trees and shrubs: if you'd like to cut material from someone's garden, then do ask permission. Similarly, ask permission if you'd like to take plant material from parks. In the countryside, removing a few stems of ivy or a branch or two of beech will not do harm, but do not take too much as it may weaken the plant.

Woodland and Hedgerow Plants to Look Out For

Willow

Willow (*Salix*) likes to grow with its roots in moist ground. It often grows along rivers or canals or on the edge of ponds or lakes. Its stems and branches are straight yet very flexible and it has been used as a basket-, fence- and garden structure-making material in many countries for millennia. Willow makes smooth, uniform wreaths, which can be used as an excellent base for adding other plants, such as ivy, wild clematis or beech leaves (you can preserve the leaves in autumn so you have them to hand in winter – see page 14 for how to do it). The flowers of pussy or goat willow are furry, grey and very soft. Wreaths made with these varieties are a gorgeous way to celebrate the approach of spring.

Herbs

Woody herbs such as rosemary and certain varieties of thyme can be used to make tiny wreaths as their stems are sturdy yet flexible, and they are brilliant as pleasantly scented, natural decorations for simply wrapped gifts, for table settings or for hanging on your tree.

Beech

Beech (*Fagus*) is one of my favourite trees. Its bark is smooth and almost silvery grey; its new spring foliage is that joyous bright acid green that announces spring's arrival; and they turn the most beautiful copper colour in autumn. This tree's bare wintry branches with their regularly spaced buds form such beautiful patterns against the sky that whenever I see this sight I find myself reaching for pen and paper. The slender twigs and branches are flexible and a wreath made from just one or two of them is simple, elegant and perfectly wintry.

Birch

Birch (*Betula*) is a pioneer species. When new land forms in a sand dune or on the edge of a fen, it is one of the first trees to grow. Its branches end in bundles of fine, very flexible woody stems that make simple, attractive wreaths. They carry small catkin-like flowers during autumn and into winter, which add texture to birch wreaths and make them a great subject for simple botanical drawings.

Ivy

This is a common wild plant species around the world and was introduced to the US by English colonists in 1727. Its young stems, which can be up to 150cm (5ft) long, cannot support themselves so the plant tends to cling to walls or the trunks of trees. Like species of clematis, its clambering habit means that its stems must be flexible, making it a perfect plant to use in wreath-making.

Hazel

Varieties of hazel tree (*Corylus*) are present on most continents, and the branches of this tree have been used to weave fences and gates since farming began. The wood of the hazel is not quite as flexible as willow, nor as straight, but the wreaths it makes are simple and beautiful, and this tree has the added bonus of bearing delicious nuts in autumn and catkins (male flowers) from November onwards. The young catkins add lovely detail to wreaths made using hazel.

Wild and Garden Varieties of Clematis

Clematis vitalba or 'Traveller's Joy' grows wild in the UK, Europe, Australia and the US and is so called because its delicate silvery seed heads cover the hedgerows in winter, making them gleam rather wonderfully in low light and offering walkers a welcome spectacle. Each seed head consists of soft, whitish hair-like fibres, giving rise to its other colloquial name, 'Old man's beard'. *Clematis ternifolia* is a wild Japanese relative of *vitalba* with similar delicate, fuzzy seed heads.

Most clematis varieties, including both wild and domesticated strains, have a clambering, twining habit and so their stems are naturally flexible. This makes them excellent candidates for making freeform delicate wreaths.

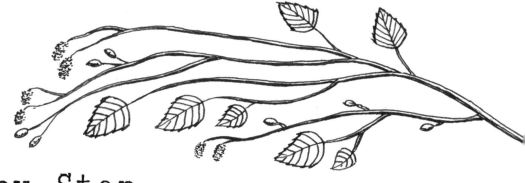

Step by Step

1   To make a large wreath for your front door or to hang on a chimney breast or wall, choose at least two twigs or stems, around 40–60cm (15–25in.) long. If you're using birch, find two bundles of fine branches about this length.

2   Cut several lengths of galvanized wire or garden twine, around 20cm (8in.) long.

3   If your twigs or stems are from hazel or willow then flex them over your knee once or twice before you begin, to encourage them to curve.

4   Lay the thick end of one of your twigs or bundles so that it overlaps by several centimetres with the thin end of another. Bind the two together with wire or twine. If you're using galvanized wire, wind it four or five times around both twigs as tightly as you can.

5   Bring the other ends of your stems or bundles together and bind again.

6   You may need to tie the twigs together at a few more points around your wreath to ensure it is sturdy and forms a rough circular shape.

7   Hang on a door, a wall or with other wreaths to make a gorgeous display.

The Greyest Days

The recent sleet has turned the garden into a muddy wasteland, and stepping outside is like an icy assault on your face and mood. There's no snow to perk up the look of your crispy perennials, your cat has become a morose recluse and your toes feel as cold as granite. It is at times like these when emergency plans are needed. A walk would require emerging from the comfort of your house and being bombarded by spikey rain or mushy snowflakes, so hibernation, contingency making and mood-boosting comfort foods are required.

I find it a reassuring thought that just a few minutes after emerging from a nest of quilts and blankets you could be creeping back beneath them armed with a mug of chocolatey, saucy joy and a spoon. My chocolate fondant in a mug is not only delicious, but the antioxidant trans-resveratrol found in cocoa has been shown to boost serotonin levels. In effect, this compound acts as a natural anti-depressant: chocolate really can cheer you up, so a lightning quick, cocoa-rich mug cake is the perfect antidote to perishing temperatures and slate-grey skies.

Gentle, meditative craft can help to distract the mind from the damp horror of the weather. The hawthorn wrist warmers are covered in little three-dimensional crocheted berries and stems.

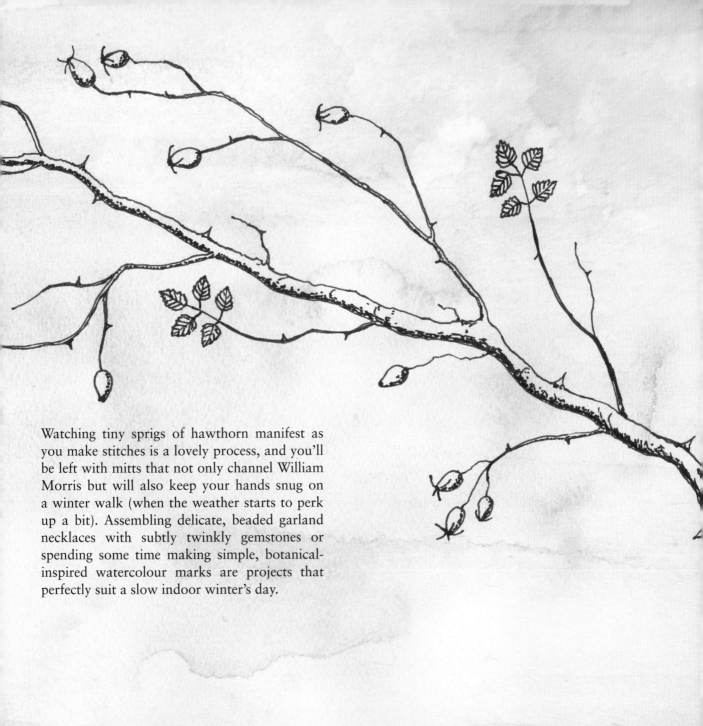

Watching tiny sprigs of hawthorn manifest as you make stitches is a lovely process, and you'll be left with mitts that not only channel William Morris but will also keep your hands snug on a winter walk (when the weather starts to perk up a bit). Assembling delicate, beaded garland necklaces with subtly twinkly gemstones or spending some time making simple, botanical-inspired watercolour marks are projects that perfectly suit a slow indoor winter's day.

5-minute Chocolate Fondant in a Mug

I'm sure you remember the feeling, or perhaps you're experiencing it now: winter has worn away your energy and all you want to do is snooze. You're craving something delicious but the thought of measuring out and mixing and then waiting for a cake to bake seems just too much. Enter this utterly brilliant recipe.

Gooey, satisfying chocolate fondant in a mug seems almost too miraculous to be true but I can confirm that this holy grail of chocolate-sauce-filled instant cakes tastes like those fancy fondant puddings you might be served in a restaurant, yet it is made from store-cupboard ingredients in five minutes (thanks to the wonders of the microwave). On a particularly grim wintry day omit the salted caramel sauce for speed, although the combination of salt-tinged liquid toffee with the rich, dark chocolate sponge and sauce may cause you to emit unseemly noises. Follow with a nap among quilts and blankets, and that bleak Sunday afternoon suddenly seems a good deal more appealing.

Ingredients

For the basic fondant mix:

3 tbsp plain flour (gluten-free flour works fine)
2 tbsp good-quality cocoa powder
¼ tsp baking powder
2 tbsp caster sugar (1½ for a slightly more grown-up, less sweet version)
Pinch of salt
2 tbsp vegetable oil
6 tbsp milk

For the optional salted caramel sauce:

90g (3oz) light soft brown sugar
150g (5oz) double cream
25g (1oz) butter
Good pinch of salt

Makes 2 small mugs-full

Step by Step

1 If you're planning on making the salted caramel, place all the ingredients for the sauce into a pan on a low heat and stir until the sugar dissolves. Then allow to bubble for 3–4 minutes until the sauce thickens. Set to one side, while you move on to the fondant.

2 Place all the dry ingredients into a jug or bowl with a pouring lip and make a well in the centre.

3 Beat continually with a whisk or fork as you slowly add the oil to the well. Then begin to add the milk in the same way.

4 Continue to whisk steadily to get rid of any lurking areas of flour. The mixture should become glossy and as thick as emulsion paint.

5 Divide the mixture between two microwave-safe mugs.

6 Drop a tablespoon or so of your salted caramel mixture (if you have made it) into the centre of the fondant mixture in your mug.

7 Microwave each mug of mixture in turn on full power (750/800W) for 40 seconds. This leaves a puddle of hot, still-molten chocolate and salted caramel sauce in the centre of the pudding. This will solidify to a delicious chocolate and toffee-ish, fudgey substance as it cools.

8 If you prefer a solid chocolate and salted caramel cake, then microwave for 50–60 seconds. It will be volcanically hot, so allow it to cool for a minute or two.

9 Pour cream or spoon a dollop of crème fraîche on top.

10 Eat with glee.

Hawthorn Wrist Warmers

Materials

2 skeins of DK yarn (approx. 200g)
4mm (size G-6) hook
Scissors
Yarn needle for weaving in ends

Abbreviations & Definitions

ch chain
sk skip
slst slip stitch
dc double crochet
tr treble crochet
yo yarn over
st/s stitch/es
tog together
dtr double treble: yo twice, insert hook, yo, pull through, [yo, pull through 2 loops] 3 times
inc increase: work 2 tr in 1 stitch
fpdtr front post double treble: yo twice, then instead of inserting hook into the top of the next stitch, poke it behind and then in front of the post of the next stitch 2 rows below and pull up a loop (4 loops on hook) then (yo pull through 2 loops) 3 times to complete the stitch. This creates a double treble stitch *in relief* on your work and resembles a cable stitch
berry tr4tog: * yo, insert hook into stitch, yo, pull through, yo, pull through two loops; rep from * three more times; yo pull through all 5 loops on hook

If the outside really seems just too dreary and grey to face, then staying indoors and conjuring some berries with hook and yarn comes a close second to seeing the real things growing in a hedgerow. This pattern is a challenge but once you have established the central and right-hand stems, there is a rhythm to the pattern that is engrossing and pleasing as the branches and berries appear. Also, as it's a pattern that needs a good deal of concentration, it is particularly good at diverting the mind away from daily stresses.

I used a skein of Eden Cottage Yarns Bowland DK in Misty Woods for my wrist warmers. It's the colour of lichen, soothing to the eye and kitten-soft. Beautiful artisanal yarn like this increases the aesthetic joy of making an item by hand. Once your wrist warmers are finished, not only will your hands be exquisitely swaddled but you may just find yourself finally equipped to face the outdoors. Of course, whether you choose to venture past your threshold or simply sit back and admire your new mitts wrapped around a mug of something steaming is another matter.

Stem Stitches

tr/fpdtr: to work this stitch you will be combining a treble worked in the next st with a front post double treble (fpdtr) worked around a st 2 rows below, as follows: yo, insert hook into next st and pull up a loop, yo, draw through 2 loops (2 loops remain on hook). Without completing the treble, yo twice, insert hook around the front post of specified st 2 rows below and pull up a loop. [Yo, pull through 2 loops] twice, then yo and pull through all 3 loops.

Central Stem (CS)

CS: tr/fpdtr in next st, working fpdtr around CS dtr 2 rows below (directly below next st).

Right-leaning Stem (RLS)

RLS (part 1): tr/fpdtr in next st, working fpdtr around CS dtr 2 rows below (to the left of next st).

RLS (part 2): tr/fpdtr in next st, working fpdtr around RLS (part 1) dtr 2 rows below (to the left of next st).

Left-leaning Stem (LLS)

LLS (part 1): tr/fpdtr in next st, working fpdtr around CS dtr 2 rows below (to the right of next st).

LLS (part 2): tr/fpdtr in next st, working fpdtr around LLS (part 1) dtr 2 rows below (to the right of next st).

Note on beginning chains and joining: When working the wrist warmer, rounds of treble and double crochet are alternated. Dc rounds begin with 1 ch, which does not count as a st; tr rounds begin with 3 ch, which do count as 1 st. To join at the end of dc rounds, slst in first dc of round; to join at the end of tr rounds, slst in third chain of 3ch.

Right Hand Wrist Warmer

To begin, work 40 foundation chain quite loosely. Join with a slst to work in the round, being careful not to twist the chain.

Round 1: ch1 (does not count as st throughout), dc in each st to end, join with a slst in 1st dc.
Round 2: ch3 (counts as 1 tr throughout), tr in each st to end, join with a slst in 3rd ch of 3ch.
Round 3: As Round 1.
Round 4 (RLS and CS established): ch3, tr16, tr/fpdtr working fpdtr around tr 2 rows below and 2 sts to the left of next st (RLS [part 1] established), tr1, tr/fpdtr working fpdtr around tr 2 rows directly below (this should be the same tr as RLS just worked – CS established), tr20, join with a slst.
Round 5: As Round 1.
Round 6: ch3, tr13, work berry in next st, tr1, RLS (part 2), work berry in next st, tr1, CS, tr20, join with a slst.
Round 7: As Round 1.
Round 8: ch3, tr15, work berry in next st, tr2, CS, tr1, LLS (part 1), tr18, join with a slst.
Round 9: As Round 1.
Round 10: ch3, tr18, CS, tr1, work berry in next st, LLS (part 2), tr1, work berry in next st, tr15, join with a slst.
Round 11: As Round 1.
Round 12: ch3, tr16, RLS (part 1), tr1, CS, tr2, work berry in next st, tr17, join with a slst.
Round 13: As Round 1.
Rounds 14-21: Repeat Rounds 6-13 once.

Round 22 (increase round): ch3, tr5, inc in next st, tr4, inc in next st, tr2, work berry in next st, tr1, RLS (part 2), work berry in next st, tr1, CS, [tr4, inc in next st] 3 times, tr5, join with a slst (45 sts).
Round 23: As Round 1.
Round 24: ch3, tr17, work berry in next st, tr2, CS, tr1, LLS (part 1), tr21, join with a slst.
Round 25: As Round 1.
Round 26: ch3, tr20, CS, tr1, work berry in next st, LLS (part 2), tr1, work berry in next st, tr18, join with a slst.
Round 27 (thumb gap round): ch1, dc in each st to last 13 sts, ch7 loosely, sk next 12 sts, dc1, join with a slst .
Round 28: ch3, tr18, RLS (part 1), tr1, CS, tr2, work berry in next st, tr in each st to end (working 7tr across 7ch of previous row), join with a slst (40 sts).
Round 29: As Round 1.
Round 30: ch3, tr15, work berry in next st, tr1, RLS (part 2), work berry in next st, tr1, CS, tr18, join with a slst.
Round 31: As Round 1.
Round 32: ch3, tr17, work berry in next st, tr4, LLS (part 1), tr16, join with a slst.
Round 33: As Round 1.
Round 34: ch3, tr22, work berry in next st, LLS (part 2), tr1, work berry in next st, tr13, join with a slst.
Round 35: As Round 1.
Round 36: ch3, tr23, work berry in next st, tr15, join with a slst.
Round 37: As Round 1.
Round 38: As Round 2.
Round 39: As Round 1.
Break yarn and weave in ends.

Left Hand Wrist Warmer

To begin, work 40 foundation chain quite loosely. Join with a slst to work in the round, being careful not to twist the chain.
Work Rounds 1-26 as for RH wrist warmer.
Round 27 (thumb gap round): ch1, dc1, ch7 loosely, sk next 12 sts, dc in next st and each st to end, join with a slst.
Round 28: ch3, tr13, (working 7tr across 7ch of previous row), RLS (part 1), tr1, CS, tr2, work berry in next st, tr20, join with a slst (40 sts).
Round 29: As Round 1.
Round 30: ch3, tr10, work berry in next st, tr1, RLS (part 2), work berry in next st, tr1, CS, tr23, join with a slst.
Round 31: As Round 1.
Round 32: ch3, tr12, work berry in next st, tr4, LLS (part 1), tr21, join with a slst.
Round 33: As Round 1.
Round 34: ch3, tr17, work berry in next st, LLS (part 2), tr1, work berry in next st, tr18, join with a slst.
Round 35: As Round 1.
Round 36: ch3, tr18, work berry in next st, tr20, join with a slst.
Round 37: As Round 1.
Round 38: As Round 2.
Round 39: As Round 1.
Break yarn and weave in ends.

If you're a beginner and would like to learn the basic crochet stitches, you can find full instructions on my website: silverpebble.net.

Beaded Garland Necklace

You may have noticed that I rather like plants. I draw them, press them into silver clay, record the progression of flowering species in the hedgerows near our cottage and even fashion them out of paper. If I could make a hat out of pussy willow or cow parsley and wear it to the supermarket without being laughed at, I would.

I've been making and selling jewellery since 1997 and one of the first necklaces I made was a tiny garland of gemstone beads hanging from a delicate chain. The beads were equally spaced, and as I added each one, the design began to remind me of tiny berries along a stem. I went on to make many of these simple garland necklaces and sold them at craft fairs and online.

Learning to attach a bead to a chain doesn't take long, and, once the steps are mastered, there are innumerable combinations of freshwater pearls, gemstones and glass or metal beads that can be used to make a range of necklaces (and bracelets if you choose a shorter chain) that any pirate would covet. Attaching just five tiny freshwater pearls or facetted garnets in the centre of a delicate chain will make a truly beautiful necklace. If I was given one as a gift, I'd be cock-a-hoop.

Materials

Snipe-nosed pliers
Round-nosed pliers
Wire cutters
Delicate silver or silver-plated chain with individual links 2–4mm (1/8in.) wide. Search for 'minibelcher' chain when ordering online
Ball pins (also known as headpins – silver-plated or silver lengths of wire 25–38mm (1–1½in.) long and 0.5mm in diameter, each with a tiny ball at its end*)
Your choice of beads (gemstones, freshwater pearls, silver or glass)

*Note: the holes drilled through most gemstone beads are around 0.5mm wide. If you buy ball pins that have a larger wire diameter than this, they may be too thick to thread through your beads. When ordering online search for ball pins that are 0.5mm in diameter (also described as '26 gauge').

Step by Step

1 Find the centre of your chain by closing the clasp and then holding it at the clasp and allowing the chain to fall free. Then pinch the chain in the middle. You can mark that central link with a little loop of wire or cotton thread to aid the later steps.

2 Thread each of your beads onto its own ball pin.

3 Grasp a ball pin with a bead threaded onto it with your round-nosed pliers, about 3mm above the top of bead.

4 Hold your round-nosed pliers so you are looking down their 'noses'.

5 Push the bead and the part of the ball pin that's below the pliers to the left slightly – to about '7 o'clock', if you were looking at a clock face.

6 Push the top, wire-end of the ball pin fairly tightly around the right-hand rounded 'nose' of the pliers so that it passes in front of the bead, essentially locking the bead in place and creating a loop of wire just above it.

7 Take the looped ball pin and bead off the pliers. Hook the wire end of the ball pin through the central link of your chain. Pull the wire so that the loop you have made is sitting in that link.

8 Using your snipe-nosed pliers, grip the wire loop you have made across its centre, ensuring the chain drapes freely behind the loop.

9 Using your fingers, twist the wire end of the ball pin around the central wire of the ball pin to form a tight spiral. Continue making the spiral until the wire just touches the top of the bead.

10 Use your wire cutters to snip the excess wire at the end of the ball pin away from the bead.

11 Use your snipe-nosed pliers to pinch the end of the wire you've just cut, so that it won't scratch your skin when you wear the necklace.

12 Repeat steps 3–11 for the next bead, inserting it a few links away from your central bead.

13 If you'd like your garland necklace to resemble berries or buds on a stem, then keep the spacing between your beads consistent – count the links before you add each bead. Alternatively, you can randomly space your beads.

14 If you're making the necklace for yourself, then trying it on and admiring it in the mirror is a critical final step.

Mark-making with Watercolours

When I was quite small, I had a watercolour set, and until I was about thirteen I painted fairly regularly – simple landscapes, patterns and studies of birds from photographs in books. As I began to study for my school exams, art disappeared from my school timetable and it seems that I stopped painting at home, too. I have no paintings made during my teens. I revived my watercolour painting for a brief period at college but other than that I had hardly picked up a paintbrush until last year. When I did, I remembered the sensation of being entirely immersed in the mixing of colours and the making of marks on paper.

It has been shown that when mammals make repetitive movements their serotonin levels increase.[1] It is likely that this applies to humans and may explain some human behaviours, such as parents rocking their children to sleep. Small tracking movements made by the eyes and the hands during creative activities seem to have beneficial and soothing psychological effects, which may also be linked to the release of feel-good neurotransmitters. One creative way of triggering this soothing effect is by painting. There is a repetitiveness to the actions required while painting with watercolours in particular – dip paint in water, brush it onto paint, touch the brush on to the palette to deposit the paint, rinse brush, repeat and mix in the palette until the desired colour is created. Making the paint marks on the paper also requires the hands and eyes to move gently backwards and forwards as the paint is transferred from the brush to the paper's surface.

As with drawing, it is easy to feel that the paintings we may make won't be worth seeing, that there's no value in even beginning because they will never end up in a gallery. But that's missing the point. The ability to be creative was crucial to our survival as hunter-gatherers, and then as Stone Age and Bronze Age humans, and was selected for over many generations. Making marks on rocks or the walls of caves, or in the soil or sand to communicate to another human being was essential for our ancestors. Picking up a brush, mixing a paint colour and using that brush to make even the simplest marks on paper taps into something ancient. That something may have become very quiet indeed over the course of many generations but can be awoken. The process of making brushstrokes can help to drown out life's noisy treadmill and dial down stress levels. The feeling is similar to that experienced during meditation or yoga.

Rows or clusters of brush marks or very simple shapes are a great place to start with watercolours. Choose a single colour and change the intensity of it as you make more marks.

Think of the colour gradation in a rainbow or colour wheel, choose your favourite two or three colours and remix your paint colour every few strokes so that your watercolour pattern develops a pleasing subtle ombré appearance.

Next, make a fine line or two in whatever colour you choose. Using a different colour, add a very simple circular or leaf shape. Several of these super simple sprigs make a very satisfying and attractive pattern. Alternatively, you can embellish them a little more. From a point a third of the way along the line from the leaf or round mark you have made, make several more lines towards that end point. Add the same simple leaf or round berry-like shape to the end of those lines too. This echoes rosehips or hawthorn berries, winter seed heads and clusters of leaves.

Another way to make a simple and beautiful botanical motif is to simply add more leaf or berry shapes on either side of the single stem you have painted. This will resemble winter buds, beech nuts or evergreen species such as cotoneaster.

1. Research by Dr Barry Jacobs of Princeton University has found that repetitive movements in mammals, such as the licking of fur, enhance the release of serotonin, associated with lifted mood. http://www.sciencedirect.com/science/article/pii/1044576595900047

Looking Ahead to Spring

Until recent years, I viewed the seasons as discrete collections of months, each inducing distinct feelings – spring: hope; summer: contentment; autumn: trepidation; winter: gloom. To my shame, I have rarely gardened during the winter months and the perennials from any particular summer are often still there when spring arrives, in desperate need of secateurs and a bonfire, all crispy and forlorn. I used to connect gardening and nature with warmer, sunnier months, neglecting my trowel entirely when the leaves started dropping, and barely glancing at hedgerows or woods because they were not filled with primroses, cow parsley or cherry blossom.

I realize that this was foolhardy. The seasons are not separate like the rooms of a house. They blend subtly into one another and sometimes there are encouraging signs of an approaching season to be found six months or more before it arrives. I began to realize that planning spring and summer activities in the midst of the colder weather can be very heartening. Seed catalogues are things of beauty and are filled with colour: marigolds and tomatoes, cornflowers and kale. Shopping for seeds is (almost) guilt-free: bulbs cost less than a fancy frock and planting them in pots indoors will ensure that you bring spring forward and have a gorgeous floral display for the New Year.

Overlooking tiny catkins and tentative baby shoots was daft, but what I also didn't realize was that digging itself can be beneficial. The gentle exercise of pushing spade or trowel into soil and the sunlight in the garden will boost serotonin, which will lift mood, but recent research is beginning to show that exposure to soil bacteria can also raise the levels of this mood-boosting neurotransmitter. If you can face the chilly temperatures, then contact with the soil itself can be an antidote to the greyest of days: getting muddy (and admittedly a bit cold) among the winter flower beds is a good thing.

Bulbs for New Year

There's a period of two months or so between the weeks leading up to the festive season and the earliest signs of spring's arrival in February, when colour is at its most scarce in the countryside. Most of the berries have been eaten by birds, the previous year's flowers and autumn leaves have died away, and the earliest blossom and blooms are yet to emerge. It's drear. There are some winter-flowering plants that can provide spots of colour but most of these are to be found in domestic gardens rather than on a winter walk.

There is a way to bring the subtle colour of late February and March forward into late December and New Year, though. If bulbs are planted indoors in September and October and kept relatively cool and dark, they will grow more quickly than their cousins outdoors. It is possible to have the cheering yellow of narcissi, the subtle blue of grape hyacinths and the simple white bells of snowdrops flowering indoors in January and, in some cases, late December – it's your very own early spring.

Materials

Spring bulbs from a garden centre
Containers – anything from enamel
   bowls to jam jars or small
   galvanized buckets will do well
All-purpose compost or bulb fibre
Pea gravel or pieces of broken clay flowerpot
Black bin bag or hessian
   sacking or old fabric
Twigs and twine to support the stems

You will also need a cool, dark place in which to store your bulb containers, such as a shed, garage or room with no heating.

Choose Your Bulbs

Europe and North America:
Crocus, hyacinth, daffodil/narcissus (e.g. miniature varieties such as Tête-á-Tête and taller early varieties such as paperwhite), miniature iris (e.g. *Iris reticulata*), grape hyacinth (*Muscari*), Siberian squill (*Scilla siberica*).

Asia:
Crocus, narcissus, starflower, hyacinth.

Australia:
Narcissus, starflower, grape hyacinth, Ixia.

Snowdrops:
Snowdrops are native to Europe but can be commonly found on sale in garden centres around the world. They can be forced using this method, but it is best to make a note of where clumps of snowdrops may have already naturalized in your garden and transplant a small clump of them into a container indoors in the autumn rather than plant bought bulbs inside, as they take several years to establish and spread. Alternatively, perhaps you could swap a tray of plum blondies or a blackberry streusel cake (see pages 22 and 68) for a clump of snowdrop bulbs from a neighbour's garden.

Choose Your Container

Jam jars work well and seeing the roots through the glass is a great way to teach children about how plants grow and take up water. Old clay plant pots always look beautiful, especially if they are aged and have patches of moss or lichen growing on them. Simple white enamel bowls, dishes or mugs are good too, although they don't have drainage holes. To prevent water from pooling at the base of any enamel vessels you're using or other containers that do not have drainage holes, place a handful of pea gravel or some broken pieces of clay pot at the bottom of your enamelware and try to use bulb fibre instead of compost. Bulb fibre is very freely draining and will help to prevent your bulbs from rotting while they develop.

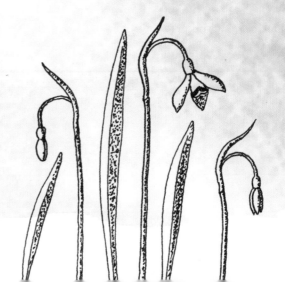

Step by Step

1 Place a layer of compost or bulb fibre in the bottom of your container (on top of the gravel or pieces of clay pot, if you are using them). Fill the container until it comes up to around 4cm (1½in.) from the rim for larger bulbs such as narcissi or hyacinths, and 2–3cm (1in.) for smaller bulbs such as snowdrops, crocuses or squill.

2 Place your bulbs on top of this lower layer. You can plant them fairly close together to create a dense display of flowers but try not to allow them to touch each other, as this might cause them to rot.

3 Cover the bulbs with more compost or bulb fibre so that just the tips of them protrude above the surface. Once the shoots emerge it is sometimes tricky to distinguish one variety of bulb from another, so label them at this stage.

4 Put your containers into a plastic or metal tray or on to individual saucers, and water them so that the soil becomes moist but not sodden.

5 Place your containers of bulbs in a cold but dryish place such as a shed, the corner of a garage or a cool cupboard that is not near a radiator. Cover the pots with a black bin bag (do not seal it), hessian sacking or 2–3 layers of old fabric or sheeting so that the light is blocked out.

6 Check your bulbs every 2 weeks or so. If the compost or bulb fibre has become dry then water it a little. Once the shoots have reached

3–5cm (1–2in.) tall, you can move your containers onto a light, cool window sill. For most bulbs this will require 8–10 weeks or so in their cool, dark spot. Paperwhite narcissi will grow more quickly and may only need 5–7 weeks.

7 Once your bulbs have been brought out into the light, avoid placing them in a very warm or dry spot, as they will need to acclimatize to the new warmer, lighter conditions. They will, however, need light to allow their shoots to develop further; 6–8 hours a day is ideal at this stage, but you needn't worry too much.

8 At this point the bulbs may grow rather quickly and become leggy. To avoid this, ensure they are near a window, but if it occurs, simply stake your plants with twigs and twine or gently wrap twine 2 to 3 times around the cluster of leaves and tie them together to provide a little support.

9 Place your pots or dishes of bulbs where they'll cheer you up most – next to your bed or near the front door so you encounter them as you come home. Your own personal, tiny version of spring is as uplifting as watching a gif of baby guinea pigs, only it's rather longer-lasting.

Hellebore Boot Cuffs

Materials

2 skeins of chunky yarn (approx. 100g)
6mm (size J-10) hook
Scissors
Yarn needle for weaving in ends

Abbreviations & Definitions

ch chain
sk skip
slst slip stitch
dc double crochet
tr treble crochet
yo yarn over
st/s stitch/es
tog together
dtr double treble: yo twice, insert hook, yo, pull through, [yo, pull through 2 loops] 3 times
2dtrtog double treble 2 sts together: yo twice, insert hook into specified st, yo, pull through, [yo, pull through 2 loops] twice; *without completing the double treble, yo twice, insert hook into specified st, yo, pull through, [yo, pull through 2 loops] twice* yo and pull through all 3 loops on hook; when working more dtr together, work as above repeating between * and * as many times as necessary, then yo and pull through all remaining loops on hook
petal 3dtrtog or [3ch, 2dtrtog] forming a petal of the hellebore motif; both of these stitch combinations are used to form petal motifs in this pattern

One of the earliest and most beautiful flowers to come into bud in late winter here in the Fens is the hellebore. The sight is as joyous to me as a glimpse of the first swallow in April. When the buds open, they always look like more of a warm-weather flower to me. The oriental varieties are deeply coloured, rather elegant and their shape is the classic five-petalled flower on a tallish stalk that I used to draw as a little girl. Unlike more subtle late-winter flowers such as snowdrops or aconites, hellebores are unmissable. They seem to shout of the approach of spring just when you've been florally deprived for three months and need them the most. I love them for that.

These boot cuffs will make your legs cosy on winter walks and will turn your wellies from functional footwear into something rather fetching. In order to closely match the colours of hellebore petals, I've used Malabrigo Mecha chunky yarn in the Lotus colourway but any soft chunky yarn whose colour cheers you up will do.

Stretch Rib Section (Worked Flat)

To begin, work 11 foundation chain quite loosely.

Row 1: sk 1st ch, dc in each ch to end. Turn.
Row 2: ch1 (does not count as st throughout), dc in back loop only in each dc to end. Turn.
Repeat Row 2 46 more times (for small-sized cuffs repeat row 2 38 more times instead).
slst ends of work together to form a tube.

Hellebore Cuff Section (Worked in the Round)

Round 1: ch1, dc in top of each row of the rib section, join with a slst in 1st dc (regular size: 48 sts / small size: 40 sts).
Round 2: ch3, sk 4dc (including st at base of ch), 3dtrtog in next dc, ch7, 3dtrtog in same dc as last petal, ch3, sk 3dc, dc1 in next dc, *ch3, sk 3 dc, [3dtrtog, ch7, 3dtrtog] in next dc, ch3, sk 3dc, dc1 in next dc; repeat from * to end, working final dc in 1st dc of previous row.
Round 3: ch5, sk 2ch, 3dtrtog in next ch, [ch3, 2dtrtog] in top of petal just made, sk [1 petal, 3ch], *dc1 in next ch (the 4th of 7ch), ch3, 8dtrtog inserting hook as follows: twice in dc just made, sk [3ch, 1 petal], insert 3 times in next ch, sk [2ch, 1dc, 2ch], insert 3 times in next ch (8dtrtog now complete), [ch3, 2dtrtog] in top of the 8dtrtog just made, sk [1 petal, 3ch]; repeat from * around, ending with dc1 in 4th of last 7ch, ch3, 5dtrtog inserting hook as follows: twice in dc just made, sk [3ch, 1 petal], insert 3 times in next ch (5dtrtog now complete), join with a slst into top of 1st petal made.

Round 4: [ch3, 2dtrtog] in top of 1st petal in previous row (same place as slst in previous row), *ch3, sk 3ch, dc1 in next dc, ch3, sk 3ch, [3dtrtog, ch7, 3dtrtog] into next st (the top of the 8dtrtog of the previous row and the centre of the hellebore flower); repeat from * around, ending with ch3, sk 3ch, dc1 in last dc, ch3, sk 3ch, 3dtrtog into same place as slst in previous row.
Round 5: ch7, dc1 into top of next petal (the 1st petal made in previous row), slst into next ch, ch3, 5dtrtog inserting hook as follows: twice into base of 3ch just made, sk [2ch, dc, 2ch], insert 3 times in next chain (5dtrtog now complete), [ch3, 2dtrtog] into top of the 5dtrtog just made, *sk [1 petal, 3ch], dc1 in next ch (the 4th of 7ch), ch3, 8dtrtog, inserting hook as follows: twice in the dc just made, sk [3ch, 1 petal], insert 3 times in next ch, sk [2ch, 1dc, 2ch], insert 3 times in next ch (8dtrtog now complete), [ch3, 2dtrtog] in top of the 8dtrtog just made; repeat from * around, ending with sk [1 petal, 3ch], dc1 in next ch (the 4th of 7ch), [ch3, 2dtrtog] in dc just made, join with a slst to top of the 5dtrtog at the beginning of this row.
Break yarn and weave in ends.

If you're a beginner and would like to learn the basic crochet stitches, you can find full instructions on my website: silverpebble.net.

How to Draw Feathers

A grey pigeon feather found on an urban street may seem like a common sight and is easily overlooked, but on close examination every feather is beautiful. A central quill or rachis is edged on both sides by delicate fibres or barbs that have microscopic hooks that interlock to ensure that the feather is able to push air downwards and create lift effectively. Feathers are small pieces of natural engineering and each one you find has been partly responsible for innumerable flights, which is rather humbling. Recently, I found something truly beautiful in our village wood: a jay's feather. It's rather small and blackish in colour, but is hatched with the most vivid kingfisher blue. It is one of my most precious nature finds.

Materials

Paper – anything will do but for
   full satisfaction value, thick
   textured paper is ideal
Your choice of pen, pencil or ink and brush
Collection of feathers

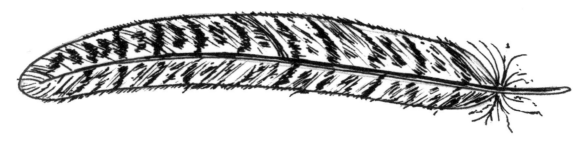

Step by Step

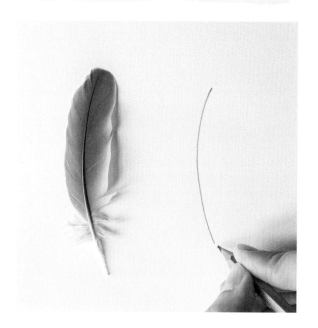

1 Take a good look at your feather in detail. The central quill is the best place to begin. Note how far down it protrudes from the bottom of the fibres or barbs and where the shaft ends. Make a mental note of the curve of the rachis and then begin. Drawing a single line for the quill is perfect for your first attempt – the main aim is not to achieve perfection, but to approximate the proportions of your feather.

2 Draw an outline of the fibres or barbs. Capturing the overall shape of the feather is the aim here – again, it does not have to look like a photograph.

3 In two or three areas along the length of the rachis draw in a few barbs. Odd numbers look especially effective. If the barbs have split from one another in one or two places, draw these triangular gaps in the barbs and erase the corresponding area of outline.

4 Add any downy or fluffy barbs if your feather has them at the base and add an extra line to widen the rachis – close to the original line at the top of the feather and slightly further away towards the quill end, suggesting increased thickness.

5 That's it! A simple line drawing of a feather. Sit back and bask in your artistic skills. Self-criticism is forbidden. If it looks a little like your dog may have drawn it (as my first feathery attempts did) then remember: wonkiness is beautiful. And practice will help – make a whole collection of feathers while out on walks and keep drawing them. Stylized, simplistic drawings can be just as eye-catching as photographically detailed ones.

Forcing Blossom

Where I live, the appearance of blackthorn or sloe blossom in the hedgerows is a key sign that the days are getting longer. In mid-February, the buds on the blackthorns begin to show as clusters of tiny pale dots against the dark, almost black, bark. The sight of them is hugely uplifting – it marks the beginning of the end of winter and acts as a cue for me to do a special, slightly embarrassing dance. The buds of several other spring blossom trees begin to swell around the same time. In the UK, forsythia and cherry plum bloom towards the end of February, but there is a way to hasten the appearance of their blossom a little. Bringing stems or branches of these species into the warmth of your house can speed up the development and opening of the flowers. If the weather is especially damp and dingy as January ends, the thought that blossom will emerge on your shelf or window sill in February can be enormously uplifting. It will help to ease your way through the final weeks of winter. Encouraging blossoms to open early is surprisingly simple, no matter where you live in the world, and can be attempted with any tree or shrub whose flower buds begin to show in late winter.

Materials

Secateurs or sturdy scissors
Branches or stems cut from spring-
   blossoming trees or shrubs
   with developing buds
Newspaper (optional)
Bath half-filled with warm water (optional)
Vases and jars in which to
   display your blossom

Keep an Eye Out

Blackthorn/sloe (*Prunus spinosa*) grows in Europe, western Asia and eastern North America. If it doesn't grow near you, simply watch carefully for flower buds to appear on trees and shrubs in your local area. Ask for permission where necessary and cut a few stems. This method works well with developing blossom buds of any species of cherry, plum or apple.

Step by Step

1 Identify trees and shrubs whose buds develop from mid-January onwards. It helps if you make a note of the blossom growing near your house during the previous spring or sloes and cherry plums in autumn, as the bare branches or stems can be tricky to identify during winter.

2 Use the secateurs to cut some branches or stems from the trees or shrubs. Don't cut too many from one plant.

3 You can simply place the stems and branches you've gathered into water and stand in a warmish, well-lit spot. Depending on their stage of development when you cut it down, the blossom should open over the course of the next week or two.

4 To speed up the process even further, half-fill your bath with lukewarm water, wrap your stems or branches in newspaper and submerge the parcel you have made in the bath. Leave in the warm water for 20 to 30 minutes, remove the parcel and unwrap the stems. Bash the cut ends of the stems or branches a little with a large pebble, small hammer or other heavy object to expose more of the water vessels (xylem) within the stems to the water in the vase.

5 Place the vase in a warm, well-lit spot and your blossom should emerge in a few days.

6 Gaze happily at the little floral snippets of spring you have brought forward in time.

Lemon, Thyme and Ginger Bars

During winter and especially in the weeks following the festive season, citrus fruit is at its best. This is also one of the most common times of year when cold and flu-like illnesses can lurk. There is some evidence that the vitamin C in citrus fruits can help to shorten the duration and severity of colds, and both the fresh ginger and fresh thyme I have included in this recipe contain compounds with proven antiviral and antibacterial properties. Together the three ingredients not only taste zingy but could also provide a baked defence against wintry ailments.

These lemon bars are a traditional American recipe and the topping is really a sort of set lemon curd or a *tarte au citron* taste-a-like. The combination of this soft, sharp layer with the crisp butteriness of the shortbread base is sure to brighten any cold, grey afternoon. Along with the plum blondies on page 22 these lemon bars make an excellent snack for a nature walk. Alternatively, eat a large slice warm, straight from the oven, with a dollop of thick cream or crème fraîche on top, a warm drink and a favourite audio book.

Ingredients

For the shortbread base:
200g (7oz) butter, softened
95g (3 oz) golden caster sugar
  or light soft brown sugar
200g (7oz) plain flour
60g (2oz) cornflour
35g (1oz) polenta (if you do not have any
  polenta use a total of 95g (3oz) cornflour)

For the lemon topping:
3 large eggs, lightly whisked
4 lemons, juiced and zested
180g (6oz) golden caster sugar
  or light soft brown sugar
25g (1oz) plain flour
2 tsp fresh thyme leaves
1 tbsp fresh ginger, grated

Makes 12–15 bars

Step by Step

1 Line a 32 x 22 x 3cm (12 x 9 x 1in.) or similarly sized square baking tray with baking parchment and preheat your oven to 180°C/350°F/gas 4.

2 Whisk or beat the softened butter and sugar together in a bowl until pale and fluffy – this should take 2–3 minutes.

3 Add the flour, cornflour and polenta, and stir into the creamed butter and sugar until the mixture forms a coherent dough.

4 Push the shortbread mixture into your lined baking tin with your fingers and up the sides a little so that it forms a uniform layer on the base and has a lip of shortbread around the edge. This will encase the lemon topping and prevent it from seeping over the edges of the shortbread. Smooth the surface of the dough with the back of a spoon. Bake the shortbread for 15 minutes until just golden. Then set to one side.

5 Place the eggs and lemon juice into a small bowl and beat them together.

6 Add the zest, sugar and flour for the lemon topping to another bowl with a lip, or a large measuring jug, and mix together. Make a well in the centre and, using a sieve, strain the lemon juice and egg mixture into it while whisking continually until everything is well combined. Add the ginger and mix to distribute.

7 To prevent the lemon mixture from slopping over the edge of the shortbread, open your oven, pull out the shelf and place your baking tray onto it. Pour the lemon mixture into the shortbread case and gently push the shelf in. Scatter the thyme leaves on top. Bake for a further 10–15 minutes until just set with a slight wobble.

8 Cut into slices, eat warm as a pudding or allow to cool and enjoy with a cuppa, or add to lunchboxes.

#makingwinter

In November 2015 I started the Instagram hashtag #makingwinter, encouraging folk to share their images of cosiness, creativity and nature. I was keen to create a soothing, uplifting gallery to which anyone could contribute and which would be a source of online creative solace and inspiration to visit on days when winter's gloom may creep in. I continued the project in the following winters and the feed now has an extraordinary collection of beautiful, seasonal photographs. There are shots of snowy landscapes, yarncraft, baking, firesides, gardening and festivities. I'm thrilled that so many instagrammers have joined forces to create such a brilliant online retreat.

I wanted to share some of them here to show just how lovely the #makingwinter feed is, should you need a little visual solace, and to encourage you to get involved, too. It was tricky to choose favourites – there were so many shots that captured the aim and essence of *Making Winter* – but I managed to narrow my selection down to the eight images shown on the opposite page. Each contributor has brought their own inspiration, subtlety and a gorgeous range of seasonal creativity to the project. Their online feeds will make your eyes happy. I thoroughly recommend that you look them up.

Left to right from the top:
@mysuburbanfarm
@lobsterandswan
@helena.moore
@marrbell
@hannahargyle
@gemmakoomen
@illyriapottery
@craftpod.co.uk

Acknowledgements

My husband, Andy, has encouraged me and cheered me on throughout the process of making this book, and has brought me innumerable cups of tea while I was balancing on chairs to take pictures of cake or swearing under my breath as I tried to wrestle yarn into three-dimensional berries. He looked after our girls when I was on a deadline and took masses of shots of my hands making things, and I'm so grateful. Hugest thanks to him.

My smallish daughters have been so patient while I've been distracted with edits, surrounded by balls of wool and hunched over a laptop. They have been my most enthusiastic cake tasters, giving each incarnation of the mug cake, the lemon bars and the streusel cake gleeful marks out of ten. The versions of the recipes that earned 12 out of 10 (or 100 out of 10) are the ones that you read here. My eldest pressed the shutter switch on my camera so many times when my hands were in shot. She's the best photography assistant.

My agent, Juliet Pickering, listened to my slightly garbled idea about crafting in winter to cheer people up over tea in King's Cross in May 2015 and told me it could become a book. Then she helped me to make it happen. She has received so many overly giddy emails from me about twigs and cakes and yarn over the past two and half years that I'm sure she must be tired by now. Thank you, Juliet.

Jemima Bicknell has tech edited every crochet pattern in this book. She has been incredibly patient, encouraging and speedy with her edits, and is an astonishing sort of wizard of the wool.

The following women, excellent pals, have been hugely encouraging and inspiring at every stage of this process, telling me I could do it, listening when I felt as though I'd never reach the end and, in Rachael's case, looking after small Mitchells so I could get the book done. They're a very lovely handmade band: Val Curwen, Sue Jones, Helen Ayres, Jane Pink, Fleur Routley, Rachael Ainscough, Charlotte Newland, Jane Duke, Sarah Phelps and Emma Freud.

Special thanks to Saul Wordsworth, with whom I exchanged hundreds of very silly tweets and who said, on the basis of a load of nonsense about bunions, 'You're a writer, you should do a book!' and to the excellent Sarah Dempster, who was my editor for a while and who said the same.

Warmest thanks to Fiona Slater, Claire Cater and the Michael O'Mara team for working so hard with me on this book and for being so incredibly encouraging. I have truly loved working with Fiona and Claire to make it a reality.

Thank you to the lovely, lovely folk on Twitter and Instagram who were very kind about my photographs and drawings and who egged me on.

Minnie, our dog, has been there by my side through hundreds of hours of photographing and typing. She was always very understanding in the small hours when I was worried about my wreaths.

Makers and Suppliers

There are many precious things in the photographs of this book that have been handmade by immensely talented designer–makers. Here are their details should you wish to buy from or commission them.

Sarah Jerath is a potter and made the beautiful mugs, pinch bowls and plates shown in this book. She digs her own clay out of the ground near her cottage and her work has a strong sense of place in its body and texture. I cherish the pieces I own that were made by Sarah. Sarah is based near Wigan in the north-west of England. sarahjerath.co.uk

Loop is the most beautiful shop I have ever stood in. Susan has created an exquisite collection of skeins of yarn and handmade accessories: it is like the cosiest cache of pirate treasure you have ever seen. Even if you don't knit or crochet, a visit to Loop in Camden Passage, London, will lift your day. Oh, and she sells online too. loopknittingshop.com

Sophie of **Grain and Knot** carves wooden spoons, knives and chopping boards by hand. Her work is gorgeously tactile yet functional and appears many times in my photographs here. Sophie is based in London and taught me to carve spoons. Her workshops are excellent. grainandknot.com

Victoria of **Eden Cottage Yarns** hand-dyes British fibres and wools in the subtlest of colours in her kitchen sink in Yorkshire. Her skeins are jewel-like and very precious, and I defy you to resist her woolly wares if you encounter them en masse at a yarn show. Her work is gorgeous. edencottageyarns.co.uk

Metal Clay sell silver clay and all the tools you may need to make your silver fossil pendant. Shayna, Jade, Stuart and the team are so supportive of new jewellery makers. metalclay.co.uk

Spoilt Rotten Beads are another of my silver clay suppliers. Juliet and the team are incredibly helpful. spoiltrottenbeads.co.uk

About the Author

Emma Mitchell is a popular designer–maker, craft teacher and naturalist. She lives in a tiny village on the edge of the Cambridgeshire Fens, where she runs nature-inspired craft workshops and creative winter retreats. Emma has been published in the *Guardian*, *Mollie Makes*, *Country Living* and Kirstie Allsopp's book *Craft*. She's also the creator and editor of *Mollie Makes Comic Relief Crafternoon* magazine, which has raised £100,000 so far for projects in the UK and Africa. She shares her joy of craft and her daily nature observations on her Instagram account, @silverpebble2, and her Twitter feed, @silverpebble. She blogs at silverpebble.net.